Raising A Child With Oppositional Defiant Disorder:

How to overcome your Childs uncooperative and hostile behavior

Rosa Newman

i

Disclaimer Notice:

Please note the information contained within this document is for educational and entertainment purposes only. All effort has been executed to present accurate, up to date, and reliable, complete information.

No warranties of any kind are declared or implied. Readers acknowledge that the author is not engaging in the rendering of legal, financial, medical or professional advice. The content within this book has been derived from various sources. Please consult a licensed professional before attempting any techniques outlined in this book.

By reading this document, the reader agrees that under no circumstances is the author responsible for any losses, direct or indirect, which are incurred as a result of the use of the information contained within this document, including, but not limited to, — errors, omissions, or inaccuracies.

About the author

As a parent of an ODD child, I can tell how hard it can be to manage a child who is easily irritable, stubborn, and simply doesn't follow the commands. The oppositional defiant disorder has a familial association, but that doesn't mean that our parents are to blame. After years of trial and testing, I finally found some scientifically proven ways to tackle my oppositional-defiant child's behavioral and emotional issues. I wanted to share the evidence-based techniques that can manage ODD children in the best way possible, along with my own ideas. This book served the purpose really well, and it can prove a savior for parents troubled by the oppositional conduct of their defiant children.

CHAPTER 1: INTRODUCTION

When mental health experts use the phrase "oppositional defiant disorder," the word that worries parents the most is "disorder." It's a word with negative overtones, meaning that the child has some illness. The parents think that they are at fault to make it even worse. I'd modify the phrase to oppositional defiant spectrum if I had the authority to change the diagnostic classifications in psychology.

What is the relevance of the spectrum? Simply said, every child exhibits oppositional, rebellious conduct at some time in their lives. Some children show it less often, and it's more accurately described as a bit of annoyance rather than a condition. On the other hand, others express it so frequently and intensely that they always have problems with their parents, school, and authorities.

This book describes how parents may assist oppositional children and improve their behavior by creating the correct situations and circumstances. Be prepared for them to reject change and to dismiss your attempts while you try to persuade them through logic and reason.

They feel that they will continue doing what they do if you ignore them. This book explains how to talk to your oppositional child and what to do if talking doesn't work.

What to Expect From Your Defiant Child

Oppositional defiant disorder (ODD) is a diagnostic term. Psychologists use it to describe young individuals who have a pattern of anger, irritation, disputing, defiance, or vindictiveness. They are of diverse ages, sizes, ethnicities, and social origins, and both sexes are represented. The Diagnostic and Statistical Manual of Mental Disorders, Fourth Edition, of the American Psychiatric Association, employs the following criteria to define their behavior:

A six-month period of negative, hostile, and defiant conduct in which four (or more) of the following characteristics are present:

· frequently loses temper.

· frequently argues with adults.

· Actively defies or refuses to comply with adults' requests or rules.

· frequently annoys others.

· frequently blames others for their mistakes or misbehaviors.

· often touchy or easily irritated by others.

· frequently angry and resentful.

· frequently spiteful or vindictive.

As children get older, they go through numerous stages in challenging your authority and questioning your most valued beliefs. It is usual for a youngster to test the boundaries set by their parents; if they do not, they will have no idea where they are. It should come as no surprise that the preacher's child, the police officer's child, and the teacher's child all go through periods of profanity, vandalism, and academic failure. Such occurrences should not be seen as parental failures. They're just the outcomes of young people pushing the boundaries of their environments.

To completely understand oppositional children's behavior, we must first comprehend how they think and see the world. I've included a few "rules" for understanding oppositional children's behavior and mental patterns below. Like any irrational or unstable thinking system, these rules should help you see that the individual is unaware of the fact that he is reaching erroneous conclusions or behaving irrationally.

You'll also notice a common thread running across all of these guidelines: The oppositional child's central ideas focus upon overcoming anybody who tries to exert authority over him. If you asked an oppositional youngster if this is how he thinks, he would most likely say no. "That's my child," most parents would answer if you asked whether this is how their children act. This knowledge will be crucial in comprehending and coping with the situation.

<u>Oppositional children and a world of superiority</u>

A dream universe in which kids constantly vanquish grownups is a much more intriguing environment for some children. "It doesn't matter what I do," one father described it to me. "I have the power to punish her, ground her, shout at her, and take things away from her. I could take everything she possesses away from her, yet nothing seems to affect her. I can go on and on until I'm blue in the face."

When a child is immersed in an oppositional dream kingdom, he might as well be in another world. Your messages, pleas, and demands appear to take an eternity to register.

For example, one young woman I worked with had black fingernail paint, jet black dyed hair, many crucifixes, miniskirts, and workboats as her unique style. "It seems like a wonderful day outside," I may say, and she'd respond, "Only if you're foolish enough to think the sun is good for you." "I hope you have a pleasant weekend," I'd remark, and she'd respond, "Fun is for those who can't think." To demonstrate that I couldn't sway her in any manner, I found little to say that she agreed with. Each of her slams, I'm sure, counted as a winning point in her head.

I couldn't take it personally because she was like this with everyone. She was, in the words of a comic I once saw on TV, an equal opportunity criminal. Whether it was myself, her parents, or her professors, she would engage in such a combative dialogue with anyone. This isn't to suggest that I approved of her. As this book unfolds, you will find that I am a firm believer in setting limits and imposing consequences for rude behavior. But I also believe that oppositional behavior must first be understood before being controlled.

<u>Oppositional optimism</u>

Rule two stems from rule one. Oppositional children view every contact with adults as a win-lose situation, and they are adamant about winning. They would not be prepared to take on adults, especially those inclined to punish them unless they had some possibility of succeeding. The hopeful dream of triumph allows children to combat so many adults. This optimism is distorted, but it is optimism nevertheless.

Oppositional optimism is frequently aimed towards achieving a specific goal. The following example shows how a child shows oppositional optimism:

"Christina's objective was to get tossed out of school in her freshman year to be transferred to alternative education. She skipped school, beat up other girls in the corridors, and had nothing but a sour attitude toward everyone who got in her way to achieving what she wanted."

Every week, Christina would show her mother a list of the people she had fought with. When she laughed, her blue eyes would sparkle, and she'd cover her lips with her chubby fingers, showing her massive collection of inexpensive jewelry. Her straw-colored hair frizzed outward, giving her an energized aspect.

Only when she recalled the week's wins, her mother would see her so enthusiastic, and she made her mother understand that joyful must be the fighter who never fails in her own mind.

<u>Oppositional children find it hard to learn from experience.</u>

Amy was unable to learn from her mistakes because she saw the world through the lens of oppositional victory distortions. She showed little to no understanding of why her parents were often unhappy with her, why her professors were lenient with her, and why she was usually the first to be blamed when there was a problem. She continued to run with a gang of friends who stole several hundred dollars in jewels from her mother one night when her parents trusted her enough to leave her at home while they went out.

In a fit of rage, her parents brought their own friends over one evening while she was out and urged them to go into her room and grab everything they wanted.

Jim was fifteen years old, dressed like an eighteen-year-old, and acted like a thirty-year-old criminal. He had a sour attitude and seemed uninterested in returning any politeness you may have shown to him. If you asked him how he was doing, he would just gaze at you and smirk. Jim was not reciprocal, in the sense that he had no more need to associate with humans than a junkyard dog. Jim regarded people as objects or services, meaning he was only interested in what you could provide him or do for him. He assumed he didn't have to do anything for you. When a psychologist first met Jim, he failed miserably in school, alienated all of his teachers, figured out how to manipulate his mother by threatening to hit her and regularly skipped school.

You can't take Jim's actions personally because you'd want to suffocate him if you did. The temptation of adults to smack youngsters like Jim (who, despite his height and thuggish attitude, could barely be regarded as anything other than a child) reveals the dark side of many people's responses to disobedient children.

According to child psychology folklore, many of the victims of childhood physical abuse are oppositional youngsters who are unfortunate enough to live with adults who cannot contain their own dreams of vengeance. This might be the source of the following regulation.

<u>Revenge is the apparent outcome of anger.</u>

A few years ago, I met with a ten years old class fellow of my son who could be characterized as a ginger-haired dynamo. He looked cute when he sat (which he didn't do very often). His attitude, on the other hand, was far from adorable. At five, he controlled his parents with his demanding, pessimistic demeanor. Their attempts to discipline or control him led to violent tantrums, name-calling, slapping, spitting, biting, and kicking. His parents, both twenty-five-year-olds, said they did not influence him.

During our initial encounter, I had the opportunity to experience his lack of control firsthand. He hid beneath one of the chairs in my dining hall and refused to come out when it was time to go back to his home. No amount of persuasion, reasoning, or bribery could persuade him to change his mind over the next few minutes.

The parents looked at me and said there was nothing they could do. I told them that I would pick him up and bring him back to the house if he was my child. After that, I'd do whatever it took to keep him there. When his father took him out from beneath the chair, the boy appeared surprised, then unleashed a barrage of ranting and threats as he walked down the hallway in his father's arms. As one could assume, he went directly for the door when he was placed in the car. Both parents glanced at me as though they had asked for my approval before dragging him back into the dining room. At that time, his demeanor resembled that of a wet tomcat. They asked me what they should do because it was clear that he would just head back towards the door if they let him go.

<u>Deep feelings are required for oppositional children.</u>

There had been an outbreak of young boys from different high schools knocking one other up. This may appear to be a regular high school rivalry, but it had taken a turn for the worst. The trend was for a group of lads to jump a boy they spotted alone, with the multiples frequently using baseball bats.

Tom had been assaulted while sitting in his car at a fast-food restaurant late one night. Someone had approached his open window, shouted "Hey!" and smacked him in the face as he turned around. He grabbed his vehicle jack handle and chased the perpetrator and his accomplices. They attempted to leave in their own vehicle, but not before Tom had dents in him.

This kind of response, in Tom's opinion, was absolutely required. It would have been cowardice on his part to respond in any other manner. Although the merits of this philosophy can be debated, it becomes a problem when a child or teenager's interactions with others are influenced by it. Tom had to use force to get what he wanted, whether punching his younger brother for not handing him the TV remote or hitting his younger sister for interrupting him. He revealed his deeper feelings and ideas centered around the need to demonstrate that no one could force him to do anything on a few occasions. He couldn't explain why this was significant, and he appeared perplexed that not everyone agreed with him. Everything seemed so apparent to him.

The best move of an odd child is to ignore you until you feel entirely helpless.

Whether or not they have heard it stated so plainly, every parent of an oppositional child is aware of this guideline. Oppositional youngsters feel that if they disregard their parents' attempts to apply logic and reason, they would be left with nothing to do. So, to speak, there are no further moves to be made. If you tell your oppositional child not to turn on the television, he is likely to assume that if he just ignores you, he will be able to get away with watching it anyhow. The loop runs like this: you speak, he misses you. He forgives you if you continue to talk. And so forth. You could quickly believe that you don't have any more options.

Dora, a rebellious fifteen-year-old whom I met after she was arrested shoplifting, tended to creep downstairs late at night, stealing the family car keys and going on pleasure rides with her buddies. Dora's parents had previously caught her taking the automobile and warned her not to do it again. They argued with logic and reason, saying things like, "You're an uninsured driver, and if you killed someone, we'd be sued for all we possess." Dora, like all rebellious children, disregarded such logic.

She seemed to believe that her parents would ultimately run out of options.

Oppositional children can't settle on something less than an adult they think they and their parents have no differences.

"If you ground me, I'll simply leave," rebellious children regularly warn their parents. There must be a thousand different versions of this remark. "You can't stop me from leaving if I want to" or "I have the right to make my own decisions."

Jennifer, who is fifteen, and a daughter of my friend, physically developed and enamored of drug traffickers and other young guys who live in the same area, says there's no reason why she shouldn't date twenty-year-old males. I wouldn't say anything if she were thirty and her partner was thirty-five, her mother claims. She claims that a five-year age gap is insignificant.

I tell her she's right in some aspects and that the gap between thirty and thirty-five may be visibly portrayed as a two-inch difference. However, the gap between fifteen and twenty is closer to two yards.

I should also mention that dating twenty to twenty-five-year-old boys is a prevalent trait among physically mature antagonistic fifteen-year-old females. Despite the sexual abuse that is common in such relationships, going out with such an older guy is an extreme indication of their status.

"What's wrong with him?" if you ask the rebellious young girls when they tell you they're dating a twenty-one-year-old.

"What do you mean? What's wrong with him?"

"Any man that age who is attracted to females of her age has something wrong with him."

"How did you get to that conclusion?"

"He'd be dating ladies his own age if there wasn't anything wrong with him."

It's easy to see where this debate may go. Jennifer will argue that she already knows everything there is to know about life and that five more years of growth and development will make no difference to her. You may dare her to approach a twenty-year-old woman and ask if she was as mature at fifteen as she is now.

Also, don't mistakenly believe that this idea of equality is limited to youth. Although it is most noticeable around fifteen, it may be noticed in far younger children. "Mother!" "You're treating me like a child," a nine-year-old recently said at a soccer game.

Her mother answered, "That's what I thought you were."

<u>Handling middle-class ODD children can be complicated.</u>

Many middle-class parents are perplexed and alarmed by their children's gangster-like behavior. For the most part, kids who were "perfect" until the horrors of hormones and rap music struck are a typical sight these days. Kids who formerly aspired to be astronauts, archaeologists, or professional sports may occasionally morph into sullen teenage barbarians with a definite lack of eye contact and a distinct disinterest in accumulating a body of knowledge.

Most parents overlook that by the time their daughters are twelve, and their sons are fourteen; they are more interested in their friends' values than their parents' ideals.

Like all other children, those with oppositional tendencies fight their parents' so-called middle-class beliefs. It's a natural period of growth, but the oppositional youngster always goes too far. The oppositional middle-class child finds all they dream about in the oppositional child from the obviously non-middle-class home's lifestyle and conduct. There is no curfew and there are no rules. There's no hovering parent in the background. Because of parental neglect, abuse, alcoholism, mental illness, and other factors, the oppositional middle-class child is envious of the absence of norms and expectations in classmates' homes, where the structure has crumbled, and the children are permitted to run wild. They feel that they shouldn't be because these children aren't subjected to any rules, demands, or expectations.

Consider your child's buddy Bob has an unusual amount of independence because his family has failed him in several ways. On the other hand, your child lacks the cognitive complexity and mental and emotional maturity to perceive things this way. I often joke with other parents that all fourteen-year-old brains are defective gadgets, especially rebellious children.

They wouldn't be astonished if all hell broke loose at home because they started a clothing and acted like gangsters if they had achieved the degree of emotional development where they could correctly think about the influence of their actions on others. They appear to feel that if their buddy Bob can act like this in his own house, they can do the same in theirs. The significant distinctions between the two situations are lost on them.

Nonetheless, the rebellious, middle-class child will try to overturn the rules and structure you've established because he feels Bob's bargain is far superior to the one you've offered him. Because they are so openly oppositional and defiant, the attitudes and actions of the child from the broken-down household appear effective in their eyes. The antagonistic child believes that acting in a very oppositional manner will lead to success. Their determined opponent effectively demonstrates to the rest of the world that no one can force him to do whatever he doesn't want to do. Such conduct is typically admired by a growing oppositional child, who aspires to replicate it.

<u>"I don't know" is the most frequent answer for oppositional children.</u>

It's something children instinctively know, even if they haven't expressed it yet. Male children show the worst responses. Ask a complicated but age-appropriate inquiry to an oppositional child. "What type of job do you want to have one day?" or anything along those lines. His eyes may glaze over, and his head may tilt back. He'll answer, "I don't know."

Children and teens who are abrasive don't seem to like thinking. To be more specific, they don't appear to enjoy thinking in analytical ways until they're debating. They go blank when asked to exchange facts or thoughts merely. They seem to limit their thinking to topics like how to satisfy their immediate desires, what type of tennis shoes are cool, who is the hottest rock or rap band, and so on. The rebellious child or teen goes too far by completely ignoring our culture's demand that people develop a knowledge base. They believe that having the right attitude is enough.

<u>Denial of responsibility is their ace move.</u>

Once again, all children are guilty of denying responsibility. And, once again, oppositional kids and teenagers go too far. One of the young girls I know has an older brother whose restored Mustang is his pride and pleasure. He let his sister drive it one night, trying to be a lovely big brother. She gathered a group of buddies, and they ended up drinking beer.

After several hours of driving and drinking, her buddies were intoxicated, and two of them puked in the car. The following day, the girl's brother awoke to discover his vehicle wet in vomit and questioned her about it. His sister, who I know to be highly rebellious and stubborn, retorted that she wasn't going to clean it up because it wasn't her who had thrown up.

How do you deal with a child like this? In the following chapters, we will attempt to address that question. But first, I'd like you to consider the structure of your family.

SPECIAL BONUS

Want this bonus book for FREE?

Get FREE, unlimited access to it and all of my new books by joining the fan base

Scan with phone to join!

CHAPTER 2: SIT BACK AND CONSIDER YOUR FAMILIAL STRUCTURE

If your child matches the behavioral patterns and attitudes described in chapter 1, the next step is to learn how to control their oppositional and defiant behavior. After that, you may assist them in changing their thinking and behavior. There is no quick way to achieve this by taking a shortcut or straight road. If this were the case, parents might simply tell the oppositional child, "I want you to alter your behavior." However, I believe that grasping structure is the foundation of all treatments for oppositional behavior.

Structure: Parents Need to Change Their Own Conduct First

Am I implying that parents must evolve? Take a moment to listen. Every action takes place in some form of context. This environment, or framework, is the home's atmosphere of expectations produced by the parents.

It encompasses all aspects of parenting a kid to be a healthy, happy, and productive adult. Rules, laws, incentives, penalties, affection, direction, and a sense of safety and security make up the structure to give us a sense of security and confinement.

You should never expect me to invite you to watch the movies in my home. Whether you came over, you may assume I was a lousy cameraman or wonder if I was living on a fault line. Many of my films have a ten-second bump in them. It seems like I was filming in the middle of a tiny earthquake.

That minor earthquake, in fact, was caused by my youngest child. If I was standing up, he was clinging to my leg from the moment he first started to walk until he was approximately six years old. He was looking for proximity, warmth, and interaction, all aspects of the structure.

The structure is best pictured as a corral, a big fence that encircles a youngster and reminds him of regularly permissible bounds of conduct. Children's nature is to test the boundaries set by structure, to see whether they can extend or overcome them.

A flexible structure is the healthiest sort of structure. When a child is performing poorly, a healthy framework swiftly closes in around him, acting as the psychological equivalent of the cavalry arriving to save the day. When he is doing well, though, it increases, ensuring that he will have plenty of areas to move around.

On the other hand, the structure might be overly tight, too loose, too flexible, or excessively stiff. Let's look at the instance of Peter. He was reared by a raging alcoholic, the kind of man who would be drunk by the time his wife returned from grocery shopping on Saturday morning, grabbing the new jar of apple juice and smashing it against a wall. He could be cheerful and friendly at his best, but his best was rarely displayed, given his drinking problem. He was rigid, dictatorial, and uncompromising when intoxicated, and he would let his son go nowhere. He'd rather have him there as a target to scold and insult. It seemed inevitable that his son would respond at some time, and retribution eventually mirrored his father's aggressive conduct. Once he became 18, he beat his father to a pulp on multiple occasions.

And then other children live in structure so expanded that it is essentially porous. In this type of structure, anything goes. Parents and children get drunk or high together. No expectations exist. If the child doesn't come home and doesn't call, then no news is good news, as they say. No academic or social expectations are made. When it comes to their fifteen-year-olds, parents who provide such loosely regulated surroundings are prone to saying things like "I just can't manage him." The difference between a good, flexibly organized child-rearing environment and one with no structure at all is the degree of control a parent is prepared to exert.

Parents who create a healthy environment for their children always think they are in charge and are eager to defend the authority that comes with their parenting position in a forceful and reasoned manner. The fact that the function of a parent is not up for grabs is one of the hallmarks of a healthy organization. The child's attempt to defeat structure is met with tolerant, amused awareness that healthy children seek power.

In situations in which tolerance and amused understanding do not work, such as with children having the drive to live outside the rules is so strong that they are immune to reason, logic, and gentle limit setting, the structure must be intensified accordingly. Many parents tell me they cannot ground their children because they will just leave the house. I point out that while the child is gone is the perfect time to go into his room and take everything of value—and I mean everything. The child returns to a room containing a mattress, a pillow, sheets, a blanket, one pair of basic jeans, two T-shirts, one jacket, one pair of shoes, a week's worth of underwear and socks, and nothing else. The parents who have gone this far tell me that by doing so, they sent a strong message to their oppositional child: "I am in charge here. If you can't accept that, you will be miserable."

When the structure is out of whack, children become symptomatic. Although problems in structure do not necessarily cause oppositional symptoms, symptoms always seem to be associated with system breakdowns. If this seems confusing, think of it this way: Cold weather does not cause snow, but the two are often associated.

It works like this: If you have a child with an oppositional personality and who is prone to challenge rules and limits, problems in the structure are likely to worsen this trait. Indeed, it seems to work the same way with other forms of psychopathology. If a child is anxiety-prone, problems in the family structure will make it worse. It is the same with depression, attention and learning issues, etc. Improvements in family structure and functioning almost always help with these issues.

When structural issues are discovered in a family, they must be addressed before the child's behavior may be expected to change. Some parents may view this as an unnecessary extra step. Why not simply tell the child that he has to change? The most exemplary case of the response is undoubtedly young children who act aggressively against their classmates at school. There are a variety of explanations for this behavior that may or may not have anything to do with family structure. In the first two years of school, children with attention issues with hyperactive behavior frequently act aggressively against their peers. Depressed kids often lash out at their classmates. Some children with a proprioceptive impairment are so sensitive that they erupt if someone merely touches them suddenly.

Regardless of the child's unique illness, practically every child I meet in my practice who hits other children comes from a family where beating and shouting are the primary forms of punishment. Parents tell me that they punish their children for striking other children at school, and they don't understand why they persist in hitting other children, as strange as it may sound. Such families are excellent examples of why a child's family structure must be reviewed before being expected to change.

Although a family's list of concerns to explore its own structure may be extensive, it's critical to focus on a few that are linked to the child's troublesome conduct. Issues such as how well the parents get along, whether married or divorced; the parents' mental health; the parents' substance use and abuse, and so on are included. Expectations of a child's behavior to change only after the structure has been inspected and determined to be sound or after issues in the family, the structure has been identified, and adequate steps to correct them have been made. The following are some ideas for parents to consider while looking at the structure they've built in their own houses.

Examining the relationship between parents and children

I'm now in contact with a couple whose daughter is often in problems at school, who seems to pick her friends based on their potential to destroy her belongings, and who exhibits many of the symptoms of rebellious children. She considers herself on par with her parents, debates everything they say, rejects reason and logic, and fantasizes about destroying authority figures. She is intelligent, yet she receives poor marks. She fights with her teachers regularly and has no idea how she affects others. She feels that others are out to get her.

The mother is a patient woman who most people would characterize as lovely and social, whereas the father is a hard-nosed realist who feels no one sees things as clearly as he does. They're in the middle of a terrible fight about finances, have been sleeping in different rooms for the past year, and openly suspect one other's motivations. They quarrel about dealing with their daughter's academic failures, poor social choices, and sexual dangers. I like to say that it takes two high-functioning adults to team up on one rebellious child. They have no hope of establishing the type of framework required to reel in their daughter since they distrust each other and act as if they don't even like each other.

"When was the last time you had any fun?" is one of my favorite questions to ask parents in situations like these. I usually observe them looking perplexed for a while before examining their memory banks. They frequently tell me that they saw a movie six months ago, or that they went out to dinner last year, or that they attended the corporate Christmas party. They tell me they've been so preoccupied with containing their rebellious child that they haven't had time for each other. I attempt to make it evident that they have little hope of controlling an oppositional child unless they operate effectively as a couple. When marital partners are dissatisfied or opposed, they will simply get in each other's way when dealing with their kids, exacerbating the problem. Before they can hope to govern their ODD child, they must seek couples counseling and rebuild their connection.

When children are caught between two fighting parents, they frequently become strategic in their own right. When mom and dad are at odds, it's simpler to gain permission to spend the week at the friend's house. When parents work together, they're far more likely to inform their daughter that no one her age stays away for a week. They also inquire about this friend and why they haven't met her and categorically state that they don't think her parents have a phone number due to religious views.

Prioritize your child over your grudges with your partner

Working together is a skill that may be used beyond the married partnership and into the divorced relationship. About half of the children I know are children of divorced parents. Almost all of their acquaintances or classmates, they tell me, come from divorced households. I'm seeing a lot of kids from reconstructed families—parents who have divorced and remarried. Some of these children come from homes where the parents split peacefully, while others come from families where the parents separated harshly. In many cases, the change in the kid is startling. Children from carefully planned divorces are often unaffected.

For example, Ryan, who was sixteen, lacked the drive to do his best in school. He and a couple of his buddies had started skipping school. He was a delightful and approachable young kid with excellent social skills, good eye contact, a well-developed vocabulary, and so on. His father told me that all of his teachers loved him and thought he had a lot of potential, but they were concerned about his recent drop in grades and attendance.

Ryan's background was unique in that both of his parents were trial attorneys who practiced a lot of family law, a field in which you are forced to deal with divorce and child custody disputes. If two parents knew how to rip each other's hearts out, Ryan's parents would know the best. Instead, they opted for a divorce that would have the least harmful influence on their child. Ryan's parents split when he was just ten years old. They decided that their child would live with his mother in the home where he had grown up and that they would work up a visiting schedule that was incredibly open and flexible. Ryan spent almost equal time with both parents when he was in his middle teenage years (other parents I know will take each other to court over being a half-hour late returning a child from visitation). Ryan's father acquired a house in the same area, only a few blocks away, so that he would have no problem going to school while Ryan stayed with him. Ryan also benefited from walking over to his father's house to see him or to his mother's house to see her when he was staying with his father.

Both parents attended Ryan's family counseling sessions. In his friendly way, he was obstinate, saying that it was his life and he should be entitled to do anything he wanted.

His parents told him that if he continued to make terrible decisions, he should expect them to work together to take away advantages like money and free time. They ensured that his existence would be monotonous and repetitive since he would have no access to cellphones, televisions, automobiles, money, friends, or the mall, among other things. Over time, he came around to their point of view.

Suppose you operate under the same assumptions as Ryan's parents. In that case, that collaboration is vital for your child — you're probably doing reasonably well when it comes to parenting your kid in a psychologically healthy manner.

<u>Check if you, as a parent, are showing violence.</u>

One of the most challenging self-examinations parents must confront while analyzing family structure is whether or not they keep their children secure. Diego, a twelve-year-old, was one of the most (literally) traumatized children I've ever known. His mother had fractured both of his elbows with a pipe. As a result, his arms were cocked out to the side as he walked. Unfortunately, his stance gave him the appearance of a classic tough person, and he was regularly asked to fight by genuine tough people.

However, overt physical abuse isn't the only type of violence that parents should know. We continue to live in a culture in which beating children is beneficial to them somehow. Children are frightened by being hit. When most parents strike, their cheeks are flushed with rage, and they appear ten times more significant due to their quickness and violent intent. If you want your child to be terrified of you and have secret thoughts of conquering you, slapping them is the best way to do this.

Many parents are frightened of being turned in to police and having their children removed from their homes if they seek treatment for their aggressive tendencies. If you are covertly aggressive and harsh to your child, it may be in his best interests for him to be permitted to live somewhere else until you have successfully transformed your views and conduct to the point that you are no longer a threat to him. It's a delicate matter to ask your state to take custody of your child while you're in therapy. I usually recommend that people considering this option consult with an attorney to ensure that they are fully aware of the law in their state. However, I am aware of several people who have done precisely this, and the courts have been relatively cooperative in working with them.

In general, judges have no desire to permanently remove children from parents who make an honest effort to change.

If you aren't violent or abusive but think you use screaming or spanking too frequently, you should talk to a therapist about parenting skills training. Parents who rely on yelling and slapping, like many therapists, usually remark that they don't know what else to do. Most child therapists can assist you in expanding your variety of options so that you have additional techniques to choose from.

Alcohol or drug addiction will prevent you from fulfilling your duty as a parent.

This is where I'm almost sure to insult or upset someone, so please accept my apologies in advance. I feel you cannot keep your drug and alcohol use while still maintaining your relationship with your child. Both of these things are mutually exclusive. For example, I recently spoke with a mother recovering from substance abuse, and she is seeking counseling for her problems. She should be commended for striving to recover from addiction, but she is still so preoccupied with it that I can't get her to stop talking about herself long enough to discuss her children. The argument is that addicts get so concentrated on their addictions that they can't see anything else.

I've seen a tendency among the individuals reared in alcohol or drug-abusing households. They knew early on, usually in the first grade, that they weren't getting the attention and affection they required from their addicted parent in some unconscious way. They get to the (again, unconscious) conclusion that if they were "good enough," the addicted parent would notice them. They would be more caring because they are children assessing the world with the naive assumption that they somehow cause everything in their family. So they do one of two things: they either give up or set out to overachieve to obtain the desired attention.

Overachievers are unlikely to have solid oppositional tendencies (they probably become depressed because they will never be able to get the attention of the addicted parent. Those who give up typically have to defend themselves against teachers and parents by being confrontational. It's important to realize that these children are unlikely to have stopped trying or quit for no reason at all. It's also worth remembering that they probably despise themselves and have little trust in their own talents.

The kids who have addicted parents frequently express doubts about their own self-worth and talents, and far too often, a crisis in the self-concept is the catalyst that takes them to a therapist's office. They have occasional suicidal thoughts, but they don't know why. They haven't pinpointed a single event that led to their demise. They simply don't like themselves and see death as a way to put an end to their misery. It's difficult enough for sober parents to deal with oppositional children. When you ask yourself to cope with one while drunk or high, you're asking for the impossible. There's also the question of what an oppositional child's addicted behavior teaches them about adults in general. Remember that rebellious children have a strong distrust of adults. When You present yourself to kids when drunk or intoxicated, it merely reinforces the idea that grownups aren't worth listening to. If you don't provide a secure framework where your attention is focused on your child, you can't expect your child to respect and obey you.

Someone else will influence your child if you don't

Susan, a thirteen-year-old girl from an upper-middle-class household, was totally normal.

She had received decent grades and had long-term friendships with girls from families with comparable values until the months before she had to see a therapist. However, Susan's father's concept of nurturing was to tell her that one more doughnut would make her "butt look like a balloon." Whether or not this is true, she feels he despises her and has no regard for her. She was desperate for a loving man in her life, but he came in the shape of a seventeen-year-old dropout with a criminal record. He declares his love for her. These remarks are a breath of fresh air for her.

I hope you're starting to consider the framework you've built for your own child at this time. Children with ODD require a robust and well-defined framework. It should be adaptable, allowing them to freely travel when performing well in school but contracting around them when they are not. It would help if you evaluated how they are not doing well since this would help make the right decisions. If your child seems to despise himself and refuses to go anywhere or do anything, he is likely sad and needs a framework that leads to treatment rather than punishment. If your child isn't doing well because she hangs out with the wrong crowd, alienates every adult she meets, and causes havoc in your home, therapy should be included in the framework.

It should, however, squeeze her in ways that make it plain that you will begin to withhold all of the luxuries she enjoys until she decides to live more responsibly. However, parents must accept several ideas and behaviors before winning this struggle. We'll look at these next.

CHAPTER 3: LET'S WORK TOGETHER ON SOME IMPORTANT IDEAS

I often ask myself what differentiates parents who have a relatively easy time dealing with their oppositional children from parents who have a rather difficult time (I emphasize "relatively"—no defiant child is simple to manage). The distinction appears to be in attitudes toward the parental role. More prosperous parents have a different perspective on their duties than those struggling. Fortunately, effective parents' ideas, attitudes, and values can be learned. They're included below with the notion that they're necessary for effectively parenting an oppositional, defiant child while also retaining your sanity.

Nothing Is Personal

Many parents tell me that they have failed their children. Their child's behavior is proof of their failure. I am confident that parents make several errors, so I have gone to such pains to encourage parents to examine their family structures.

However, I always remind parents that children have personalities and that oppositional personality characteristics are sometimes just a part of who they are. Academic psychologists spend whole volumes debating the nature of the character and how much of it is hereditary vs. taught. It's enough to state that nature and nurture appear to act in conjunction at this stage. A child is born with particular characteristics, which interact with and are affected by the environment.

I've met children who have been defiant and oppositional since birth. One of the boys I know is three and a half years old and has already been booted out of numerous daycare centers due to his constant bickering with teachers. He bullies, punches, pushes the other kids, snatches their toys, and appears resistant to the daycare attendants' sanctions (typically, they use time out or separation from the group). He is a bright, energetic, and uncompromising individual. He's as content as a clam as long as he gets his way. His grandma, who has custody of him, and another woman who has occasionally babysat him say he has always been like this.

Parents whose children were not rebellious at a young age may find oppositional conduct much more unpleasant. These are the parents of the "model" child that has just transformed into a horrible horror movie monster. The typical tale goes like this: young kids see their friends get away with outlandish behavior at school, on the playground, or in the neighborhood, and they decide to try it out for themselves. It's important to remember that we live in a time where openly defying authority is more "popular" than ever. I believe that most adults twenty years ago would have dismissed predictions of guns in high schools, drugs in elementary schools, popular music laced with the most heinous words imaginable. They can't expect nine-year-olds with the vocabularies of dock workers as a lousy fantasy from some sci-fi novel. Although it is undoubtedly possible to raise a kid to become oppositional and rebellious, most of the children I know either already has these characteristics. They may have been impacted by their peer culture and have begun to follow their oppositional mentors. Only a few of the ones I'm familiar with are entirely the result of their parent's bad habits. At some point, parents must realize that wondering where they went wrong is a waste of time. Examine the family structure, mend what needs to be fixed, and start making new expectations on the oppositional child to improve his behavior.

I'm the parent and the authority.

Stopping to get a feel of who all the participants in the game are is an essential part of building your game plan. Consider the concept of power in this case. Children and teens certainly have a lot of power, but it's an emotional kind of power. Only a tiny number of them can act in a harmful manner. For the most part, their power is restricted to bugging, irritating, enraging, and disappointing others.

Parents, on the other hand, wield legal authority. The legal control they have over a child or teenager is close to absolute as long as parents operate logically, consistently, and non-abusive. The issue is that most parents overlook this information along the way. They get down in the trenches with their acrimonious children and fight a battle from the child's emotional point of view, not the adult's legal point of view. The true challenge in parenting an oppositional kid arises when the parent's standard of behavior is lowered to that of the child.

Consider the following scenario: Your daughter, who used to be well-socialized and intellectually gifted but has recently started hanging around with bleary-eyed exploiters, tells you she wants to go to a friend's house tonight for a party and plans to stay the night. You inquire about the party's supervision and who will be present. She tells you that you're treating her like a kid since she's "like four," and she tells you she's leaving whether you like it or not. You tell her you don't like it, she's not going, and you won't allow her to approach the door if she attempts to leave. She starts yelling even louder about how everyone she knows gets better treatment and claims she'll phone her friends to come to rescue her. You start yelling about all of your efforts and all you've given her. You threaten to nail her windows shut and ground her until she's old enough to draw social security, and she threatens to report you for child abuse for shouting at her and blocking the door.

It's critical in instances like this to remember that you're the parent, and your role isn't up for grabs. It's also crucial to stay strategic and start examining the thinking flaws your daughter is making during the conflict. She is most likely fantasizing about beating the adult. She's also disregarding your requests, hoping that you'll eventually give in and order her to go.

In this conflict, she is seeking to adopt the role of your equal. She's probably seen her new friends behaving this way with their teachers at school or overheard them bragging about how they treat their parents.

It's less crucial what you do than what you don't do at this point. Allowing oneself to be drawn into a screaming battle is not a good idea. Teenagers' territory is yelling contests. Because they feel they have nothing to lose, they will win each competition. When you participate in the ranting, whatever they say will startle or hurt you more, and you will be bruised. It is in your best interests to stay a parent. "I'm sorry," you say. However, if you can't tell me who will be there and who will monitor, I will not let you go. This is not a point on which I am ready to disagree with you."

At this moment, your child has two options. She may back down and mumble under her breath, or she can escalate. If she chooses to escalate, you must remain calm and state that you have already given your answer as the parent. She may go if she can persuade you that the party is appropriately monitored, which you would check, and that the individuals going are people you will allow her to be around. Otherwise, you say, you don't see the need to repeat yourself.

That final bit was a fabrication. Here, your technique is to repeat yourself for as long as it takes gently. Your daughter may become more agitated, even throwing a full-fledged nuclear hissy fit, but you will not be defeated if you maintain your calm, parental position. Remember that you can only be beaten when you stop acting like a parent and start arguing like a teenager. Many parents have doubted this approach before they attempt it. What if your daughter claims you can't keep her at home and that if you get in her way, she'll punch you, shove you away, or climb out a window, they ask?

At this moment, parents should inform their child of two things. The first step entails: Tell her you have no intention of doing anything as naive as standing in front of a door or attempting to prevent someone from fleeing. That would be behaving adolescent-like. Her choice to follow or disobey your guidelines is entirely her own. You say she will return to a wasteland if she departs when you tell her not to. Her room will be torn down to its foundations. Everything of value will be removed, and once removed, it will not be returned if it does come back; it will only bring back a few things at a time, based only on her good conduct. If she insists on acting this way, she can say goodbye to everything you provide, including the phone, television, transportation, money, trips to the mall, make-up, having friends over, snacks.

The ability to go into the fridge and get drinks on demand will be lost.

Step two: Tell her that you will report her to the police and file charges against her if she ever hits you. Inform her that, while she is unlikely to go to jail for such an incident (unless she has a history of violent conduct), she will very indeed be placed on probation. She will have to visit with a probation officer every week. She will very indeed be sentenced to many hours of community service. Make her pay the court expenses, which will be significant. You'll demand that she pay a percentage of the counseling costs if the judge requires her to attend. Then tell her that after all of this, you're still going to do what you said you'd do in step one. Say everything in a calm, authoritative tone, and then follow through so she doesn't think you're lying.

If your daughter chooses to back down or give you the facts you need to make your choice, it is as important—and equally parental—to applaud her for making a wise decision. In this case, you tell your kid that she is acting maturely. By doing so, you are much more likely to trust her and enable her to make her own decisions.

Although you may not let her attend this specific party, her mature behavior will ensure that she has many more opportunities to make her own decisions in the future.

<u>The parents own everything in the house.</u>

It's time to express this point adequately. It's important to highlight that parents are the sole owners of their children's belongings. "You can't take away my bike," an oppositional kid will respond (can also be T.V., stereo, phone, car, whatever). That is mine to use whenever I want to use it."

I go to extraordinary lengths to explain that children under the age of responsibility and maturity cannot legally own something, even if they have paid for these things with their own money. They also have no legal claim to the items in the house that are generally for family use but are purchased by the parents.

The list of options accessible to most children growing up in a so-called middle-class family is somewhat unbelievable. I usually suggest to parents to put together a list with their children. I recommend that they compile a list of "obvious reinforcers" and "subtle reinforcers," as I refer to them. Among the obvious reinforcers are the following:

· A T.V for family and individuals

· Stereo speakers

· Cassette players

· Hands-free

· DVD

· Laptops and Desktops

· Consoles and Computer games

· Mobile phones and telephones

· Bikes

· Skates

· Cars

· Motorcycles

· Sports equipment

· Money

· Fishing equipment

· The chance to have friends to visit you or vice versa

· Access to malls, arcades, parks, and sports fields

The subtle reinforcers are things parents hardly think about monitoring, but they significantly impact ODD kids. This includes stuff like:

· The ability to have a long shower or bath

· Access to favorite t-shirts

· Shorts

· Jeans

· Jackets

When punished, they can't wear any clothes that are associated with designer brands, sports teams, music bands, or other logos. You can also include access to refreshments, the right to have photos and posters on their rooms' walls, access to collected stuff (sports cards, coin collections, model cars, and planes), the chance to have a part-time job, and so on, depending on the circumstances. The parent should inform the child that the parent has access to both subtle and obvious reinforcers.

Disputes among parents should never undermine their control over the house.

When parents yell, shout, threaten, or physically lash out in anger all the time, they send a clear message: no one is in control. The effect on a child is similar to a passenger on an airplane. The person looks into the cockpit and sees the captain and copilot striking each other. And the child wonders who's in control of the plane. What's the pilot's name?

Children learn that no one controls the plane if their parents have frequent arguments. Any intelligent child will attempt to escape, doing so in several ways. Young people, in particular, are affected by depression.

They start to think of themselves as horrible children because they believe they are causing the family friction, which is their fault. Teenagers usually follow one of many paths. Teachers, strangers, or friends are the targets of their rage because of what is happening at home. To escape, they may turn to drugs, food, or something that keeps their mind away from the house disputes. By fifteen, they are engaged in semi-partnerships to start new families. There are plenty of other reasons why children try to escape. On the other hand, parents who lose control are the stewards who most clearly show the way to the exit.

CHAPTER 4: IT'S TIME TO PAY ATTENTION

Some parents eventually stop paying attention to their disobedient children. On the other hand, the majority merely go about their business, delivering unwanted attention: they overlook the child's good behavior (or pay the halfhearted compliments for it). They unknowingly encourage undesirable behavior by pressing the child's emotional buttons, enabling their attitude to dictate their reactions, and puzzling the child with inconsistent responses.

From afar, it's clear that a youngster who feels he can't earn your grin by nicely behaving isn't going to battle his rebellious tendencies very hard. On the other hand, you do not have the benefit of that distance.

It doesn't work that way, but parents become so engrossed in the pattern that they lose sight of what's going on: constant negative attention not only fails to "frighten out" your child but may also cause significant harm.

For a good reason, psychologists term their theories regarding the parent-child relationship "attachment theory." Your child is bound to look to you for approval, admiration, and acceptance from the moment they are born. Your smiles and nods reassure your baby that learning to stand and walk is crucial—even if it means risking a fall. Your praise for how well your child draws or tosses a ball straight reassures her that she is a person deserving of affection. Even when he misbehaves, your patience, forgiveness, and understanding show your child that he is loved.

You lose a lot more than an excellent weapon for obtaining your child's cooperation when they stop respecting your attention.

You betray the kid's trust, sever an irreplaceable link, and forego a piece of your ability to guide the child to happy and healthy adulthood.

That's why it's critical to relearn how to give your child the attention they deserve, which is the purpose of this chapter. The first step's crux is a deceptively basic approach known as "special time," which provides surprisingly significant benefits:

It will show you directly that how you react to your child has a significant impact on how motivated your child is to do what you ask, whether it's making a bed or not striking other kids.

Rather than the other way around, it will educate you to identify and acknowledge excellent conduct while ignoring undesirable behavior.

It will teach you to value your child and your time together. It will begin to heal the scars of frequent conflict, re-establish trust, and re-establish a willingness to serve one another.

Of course, if you merely try half-heartedly to learn this step, you won't get these rewards. Many parents incorrectly believe that paying good attention is straightforward because it seems simple. It's not the case. You have a lot of habits to unlearn when you've been locked in a vortex of confrontations with a disobedient youngster. The only way to get the above benefits is to take this step exceptionally seriously. The only way to make the following action effective is to gain the above benefits. Step 2 will teach you to use praise to elicit collaboration, which won't work if your cheers are constantly interrupted by booing.

What Type of "Boss" Have You Had?

Make two columns on a sheet of paper and write "Worst Supervisor" at the top of one of them. Make a list of five traits of the worst boss you've ever had under that topic.

What was your experience with that boss?

Now think about how you worked for your worst boss. With enthusiasm or reluctance? Is it better to work as hard as possible or as little as possible? With bitterness and deception, or with compassion and loyalty?

Write "Finest Supervisor" at the top of the opposite column on your sheet of paper, and then repeat steps 1–2 for the best supervisor you can recall.

Now take a hard look at both lists and decide which column best describes how you treat your child. Be truthful.

<u>Have a special time with your child</u>

Make "special time " —15 to 20 minutes devoted just to have a relaxed playtime with your child—a part of your day to become your child's greatest potential "boss."

 Your objective is to learn to focus on the positives—your child's good conduct, accomplishments, abilities, and other positive characteristics—as well as to reclaim your child's trust. I've noticed that the best way to do both is to set up a setting in which you are not allowed to provide any orders, instructions, or probing inquiries. I'm asking you to hand over control to your child, as radical as that may sound. It's simply fun, so allowing him to make his own decisions and errors shouldn't be too difficult. Here's the tricky part: no matter what's happening inside your thoughts, don't say anything unpleasant. Follow this strategy:

Look for a moment during the day when your child is doing something you know they love, when you have 15 or 20 minutes to spare and nothing pressing or stressful to do after that. Join the child without any drama, whether it's standing outdoors at the basketball hoop or sitting on the floor among the action figures, and simply start observing. Allow yourself a few minutes to thoroughly scan and make mental notes. What is your child up to these days? I'm curious as to how long he's been doing this.

Is this an extension of a game or project that the child started a few days ago or a brand-new activity? Is there a goal, or is it merely for the sake of having fun? Is the child ecstatic or completely absorbed? Is it better to plan ahead or to improvise? You might feel compelled to ask the child to explain what's going on, but avoid the temptation. Disrupting a child's play, even with basic questions, might lead to the standard "Mom or Dad in control" scenario.

Now you may start making observations about what your child is doing. Keep your comments short and sweet. Don't be too sentimental, forced, or false. Simply show genuine interest in what your child is doing and, when appropriate, punctuate your narrative with genuine praise. If your child is shooting baskets, you may start by saying, "Nice shot!" and then move on to more detailed information to demonstrate your genuine interest: "So, you're putting in a lot of practice time on your outside shot... You're improving your rebounding skills... I believe it's fantastic that you're putting so much effort into this..." You can also choose a more lively option. "And he goes up for the layup--two points!" says the "sportscaster" who is actually doing the "play-by-play." "And he goes up for the layup--two points!" He dribbles back and attempts an outside shot." In fact, many parents have discovered that this broadcasting technique works well with many types of play. After 20 minutes, tell your child how much fun you had playing together and that you'd want to have a "special time" to do it every day.

In two-parent families (or indifferent houses where the parents live), both of you must set aside a particular time, preferably five days out of the first week. Up until adolescence, special occasions should be a staple of your relationship; however, as time passes, you can limit the frequency to three or four days each week. Don't be shocked if you and your child like these sessions so much that you'd want to have them more frequently rather than less frequently.

Keep a short record of your experiences and observations on special occasions over the first week—what you two did together, how it went, and any changes you saw in your relationship.

<u>Best time for a special time</u>

It's typically reasonable to set up a regularly planned time for children under the age of nine, whether it's when older siblings are at school, after school, or supper for a school-age child.

Make sure it's a time that's convenient for both of you when you'll be comfortable and ready to give your full attention to your ODD child. Your focus will be split, and its effects lessen if you're concerned with other duties, such as beginning or returning to work or home tasks.

You'll have to be a little more flexible with children beyond the age of nine. Children's calendars begin to fill up around fourth grade, and you'll have to seize chances when they arise. Stop what you're doing and start an unplanned special time with your child when you find them happy playing alone.

<u>Best time for play</u>

Whatever the child chooses is the best form of play—no, the only type that is acceptable for a special time. When the planned time arrives for children under the age of nine, simply go up to your child and say (in your own, natural words)," "It's now our turn to have some fun together. What do you want to do?"

Go ahead and participate if you can do so without being overbearing in any manner, especially if your child begs you to. Take a backseat, though, and allow the child to lead the action.
Otherwise, just be a kind friend and a curious—even fascinated spectator.

Some defiant children will try to take advantage of their newfound freedom of choice since they are used to being restrained. One clever six-year-old insisted on coloring on the walls with his mother. Of course, this was absurd. On the other hand, the mother outmaneuvered him by taking some butcher paper, attaching it to the wall, and then coloring the paper with her kid. They even kept their mural up for a few days so that everyone might see it. Saran Wrap, she said, may have worked as well.

By promising to drive his curious 12-year-old about as often as possible, one parent was able to entice her into a special time. Then, when the girl turned up the volume on the radio, Dad kept his cool and made neutral comments about the music instead of yelling or insisting she turn it down. He said that it didn't take long for her to become more interested in spending one-on-one time with him. You'll have a hard time breaking your negative conduct habits unless you're prepared to give up control for this brief moment of goodwill. If you can't bend sufficiently to appreciate the time spent with your child even when you don't like the activity, an evaluation of your own "risk factors" could be in order.

However, allowing your child to select does not imply that you will be mentally prepped for a special time. Some tasks will be simpler to resist instructions and questions than others, and you should be aware of which ones are likely to urge you to take leadership. Perhaps you have a skill or ability that you'd like to share? When their special time involves creating a story, one editor I know had to clench her teeth to avoid correcting her daughter's English. "No, you do it this way," a graphic artist says as he clenches his fists to avoid snatching his son's paintbrush.

I often tell parents that there is nothing they need to teach their child that they can't wait till later. Remembering such advice may assist you in resisting the want to guide or correct your child during "dangerous" activities. Other "threats" may be more difficult to foresee. To my amazement, I've heard parents confess they couldn't prevent themselves from intervening because they, too, wanted to participate. Remember who's in control during the particular time before you intervene, "Hey, it's my turn." There are no regulations in this situation. In fact, if your child has selected a competitive game, don't hold it against her if she makes up new rules or even cheats.

Finally, the one thing I would avoid for a particular time is watching television. There isn't much to look at, and "narrating" a television show would irritate even the most sensitive youngsters! Of course, many children's first inclination is to turn on the television. We usually advise parents to persuade their children to choose something else or just reschedule the particular time for when the child's favorite programs are not broadcast. A few parents have let their children choose what they want to watch on TV and turned it into a snuggling time with some talking, but I still believe the full benefit of attention is lost.

CHAPTER 5: PEACE THROUGH PRAISE

See for yourself when your child is good.

You already know how much your child likes your attention and praise during playing if you go back to Step 1. This is your last chance to test how this positive consequence affects compliance. The key to this strategy is to be rapid; when you answer quickly, your attention will be drawn in more thoroughly. The first lesson you'll learn is to pay close attention every time your child follows your instructions.

Instead of stepping away to attend to your own business when you give your child a command—whether it's "Brush your teeth," "Do your schoolwork," or "Stop pulling the dog's tail," as most of us do—stay with the child and watch.

If the child continues to disobey, treat the situation as you normally would. Don't attempt to invent new ways to punish your children. If the child begins to obey, acknowledge it right away: "I appreciate it when you do what I ask," for example. "Look at how well you're...," and "Thanks for..." are just a couple of examples of what you might say to encourage the child's cooperation with positive attention.

If you absolutely must leave the room, do so briefly but frequently return while the work is being completed. Continue to lavish praise on your child as long as they follow your instructions.

For nearly every command you issue, follow these instructions.
When you catch your child doing something extraordinary without being asked, add a modest reward — a small toy, favorite food, or extra privilege. Even stubborn children are capable of doing the right thing on their own. One parent was astounded to see his five-year-old son, who had been complimented on his laundry assistance, put everyone's laundry away for the remainder of the week. You want to follow home rules without being reminded or complete a duty without parental instruction. Then it would help if you didn't allow these accomplishments to go unrecognized. Make a good impression!

Show your child how easy cooperation is

You can genuinely teach your child to obey by simple repetition, believe it or not. Just like how quickly you learn an exercise routine is mainly determined by how often you do it, how successfully your child develops the compliance habit is primarily determined by how often they get the opportunity to practice.

The second strategy to employ is to create a "cooperation workouts" routine.

Find at least two or three periods during the day when your child is not very engaged with exciting activities that they will dislike when being interrupted. These can be around the exact times every day for a small child with a regular schedule; with an older child, you'll have to keep an eye out for chances.

Over the following three to five minutes, provide a set of five or six orders. Keep the orders brief and easy to understand: "Please pass me that book"; "Can you reach that pencil on the table for me?"; "Please close that window curtain"; "Turn on that lamp"; and so on. Each instruction should only need a few seconds of your child's time and effort.

Praise your kid as they comply with each request, just as you would for routine requests made throughout the day.

• *A modest reward such as a favorite meal or drink can be given to very young children as a reward.*

• *Verbal gratitude should be enough for older children.*

<u>Compelling commands and orders</u>

In my years of working with my ODD children, I've discovered that merely changing the manner you offer instructions and requests may enhance your child's behavior significantly. Work on tailoring your orders for the best impact while you're remaining around to follow through on demands so you can congratulate your child for participating. To assist you, here are six stages and two tools:

Six Steps

Make sure you're serious. Many parents react angrily to this advice, saying, "Do you honestly think I'd put myself in the position of putting unwarranted demands of a child who already doesn't obey?" I'm sure you're not aware that you're making unnecessary asks of your child—and that's precisely the purpose. Some parents of oppositional children become so disheartened that they give up and stop paying attention or making requests. The causes behind this are unclear. Maybe it's an unconscious type of experimentation—"Let's throw everything we've got at this problem and see what sticks"—to discover which orders are a problem. It might also be a desperate attempt to make yourself seem more competent by getting your child to follow a command.

In any event, offering more directions merely provides your child and you more chances to "fail" unless you're ready to follow the instructions in this chapter. As a result, the first thing you should do while issuing standard orders is pause and consider the command's relative relevance before giving it. Is this a top priority for you? Is it something your child is now required to do? Most importantly, are you prepared to remain around and see things through? Don't say anything if the answer to any of these questions is no. Put off the work or completely forget about it. If you get a yes, be ready to back up anything you ask with positive and bad outcomes. Compliance will increase with time as your child realizes that you mean every instruction you issue.

This type of phrasing quickly informs the youngster that they can refuse to cooperate, and you may return to additional politeness once your child has established a strong habit of cooperating. Make your request an introductory remark for the time being.

Maintain a straightforward approach. Almost all children, particularly younger ones, will be perplexed by a complex command or a series of commands. The typical reaction to this perplexity is to refuse to do whatever you've asked.

Even if you require your child to do numerous activities, stick to one command at a time. Wait until you've commended the child for successfully completing the first one before imposing the second. If your request is complicated, try to break it down into multiple smaller pieces that may be terminated and complimented independently (see the following tools).

Ensure that you are heard. You can't be sure your child has listened if you don't make eye contact. Many of us succumb to the urge to issue a directive from another room or continue doing what we're doing without looking up.

Getting Rid of the Competition is a must. Another strategy to ensure that the kid hears you is to turn off all other sources of distraction, such as the television, stereo, video games, or anything else that is likely to compete for the child's attention. You can instruct your child to turn off these distractions, but many parents would instead do it themselves, so they don't have to give a command before getting to the topic.

Double-check that you've been understood. Ask the kid to repeat the command if you don't believe the child has heard and comprehended what you want—the child stares at you unblinkingly with a hazy look on their face, does not respond, or makes no eye contact with you. This appears to be especially beneficial for children with short attention spans, such as those with ADHD and ODD.

Useful tools

Set a timer for yourself. Any reminder that "time is of the essence" can motivate the child to get started. Therefore, many parents find it quite beneficial to inform ODD children how much time they have to do the work and then set a timer for that duration. Of course, if you want to do this, you will need to follow up. What will the child get if they finish the assignment in the allocated time? What will the consequences be if you don't comply?

Make up a chore list. Making out chore cards for children who are old enough to read and assigned regular jobs or other responsibilities helps the kid keep on track and avoids any disagreements about what you meant when you asked your daughter to "clean up the kitchen after supper" for example.

Simply write out the procedures required to complete the project in sequence on three-by-five-inch file cards. While performing the task, the child can carry the card around as a reminder. Some parents find it beneficial to include a time restriction for the entire work (or even for specific steps) and use the timer in conjunction with the chore cards.

<u>Reducing the interruptions</u>

I needed help with housework and errands all day, and Mick was nowhere to be seen. He had miraculously vanished by the time I had time to go through his assignments with him. Why is it that only when I'm attempting to make a phone call, pay bills, or read a book does he appear to be all over me?

Parents with disobedient children sometimes lament their inability to get things done without interruption. When you can't chat on the phone, do paperwork, talk at the dinner table, read, or watch TV without being interrupted, the aggravation of having your commands ignored, your warnings ignored, and your wants opposed exponentially.

On the surface, Mick's actions appear to be contradictory. It's not that difficult to comprehend when you look at it as another element of the attention problem. It's also not difficult to change in that light.

Because he gets recognition for interrupting your chats and upsetting your work, your child will continue to do so—but not for leaving you alone. When your child keeps bugging you while you're attempting to make supper, you may scold or shout at him. When Jessica doesn't stop screaming in your other ear when you're chatting to a buddy, you could even cut your phone conversations short. "All right, Bob, why don't you tell us about your day if you really can't wait," you and your spouse can say when your young kid won't let you catch up on each other's day at the dinner table.

The answer should be self-evident: To persuade the child to leave you alone, make it more tempting. When the child is not interrupting, pay attention and ignore the child's effort to butt in. Giving the child something to do while you're busy and pausing to congratulate the child for not bothering you are both parts of the approach.

When you know you're going to make a long phone conversation, start a work that demands your full attention, or just need some quiet time, come up with a fun activity and tell your child to do it while you're busy, so you don't get interrupted.

Now begin your activity, but after approximately 30 seconds, stop what you're doing and congratulate your child on not interrupting you.

Return to your task, pausing after a minute to compliment your child on not bothering you.

Continue in this manner, extending the time between praise offers until you're done.

Choose two or three tasks that are particularly difficult for you to practice this method. Many parents find phone calls to be a significant source of stress. If you want to practice making phone calls, have a friend or your spouse call you at home a few times a day so you can do it without insulting the person on the other end of the line.

Whether it's drawing, watching TV, or playing a video game, the activity you employ to occupy your child should not be fancy or uncommon, but it should be something the child loves. It should never be regarded as a chore.

Quit what you're doing and walk over to your kid to thank her for not interrupting you; if you notice your child ready to stop what she's doing to come over and interrupt you.
You can increase the distance between compliments not just inside a single session but also from week to week.

The praise you give the child at the end of this period should be more than the praise you've been giving them regularly throughout the assignment. Consider offering a little incentive in addition to verbal appreciation.

This activity should be continued until your kid can play alone for around 10 minutes, depending on maturity. Remember, your first aim isn't to finish the activity at hand but to pay attention and thank your child for not interrupting you.

CHAPTER 6: OFFER REWARDS WHEN YOU CAN'T WIN WITH PRAISE

This is, predictably, a tool that anybody can use, and I highly advise you to use it with any ODD child aged four or older, even if your child has previously made significant progress with Step 2. This incentive system will accelerate your child's growth, move their behavior back into the typical range, and make those gains permanent. If your kid is three years old or younger, keep to quick, observable incentives for cooperation, such as a tiny snack, a sticker, or a small toy, or playing a short game together. The notion that chips or points represent rewards and privileges may be complex for small children to understand. Even if they do, their numerical abilities will make this task challenging.

You'll set up a token system in which your kid gets chips or points for accomplishing specific chores when requested and then redeems these tokens for prizes or privileges that are important to them. Why don't you make it easier on yourself and give the child something on the spot, as you do now?

Little snacks and sweets rapidly lose their appeal when you give out the number of prizes required to induce positive behavior, hence their motivational effectiveness. You'll need a range of awards, some of which are more valuable than others, and most of these can't be given out right away. You can't reward math homework completion with 15 minutes of the TV when your child still has science and reading tasks ahead of him. The solution is to keep the child engaged by instantly awarding points for compliance—a motivational incentive that can be redeemed for a specific privilege later.

Doesn't it sound like a game? It ought to. The entire process should be approached positively and presented as pleasant and beneficial. Make it fun and get creative with props, and your child will be just as enthusiastic about it.

Home poker

Get a basic set of plastic poker chips—most people already have one. If your child is just four or five years old, the white, red, and blue chips will count as one chip or point. If your child is six or seven years old, you can play poker with the chips: white = 1, blue = 5, and red = 10. If that's the case, attach one chip of each hue to a card. Mark the value of each color; this will serve as a reminder to your child.

Set aside some time to explain the system to your child in a peaceful environment. Tell your child that you don't think they have been rewarded enough for all the awesome things they accomplish at home to keep the tone upbeat.

Show your child the poker chips and explain that they will be the "money" for performing particular tasks. They will earn varying chips for different tasks: The more difficult and time-consuming, the more awarded chips. Declare upfront that the child will only receive chips if they complete the task at your first request and only when completed. "You'll still have to make your bed if I have to ask you again," you can explain, "but you won't receive any chips for it." "I asked you to make your bed, and it's great that you went in there right away to do it, but you didn't finish, so you don't get any chips this time," or, "I asked you to make your bed, and it's great that you went in there right away to do it, but you didn't finish, so you don't get any chips this time."

Choose a "bank" to hold the chips together. It can be a coffee can with a flat rim, a shoebox, a plastic jar, or another container. Allow the kid to assist in the selection of the bank. After that, you and your partner may have some fun decorating it.

Make a list of privileges now: Ask your child what they would like to receive as a reward for good behavior. Most kids will begin with the biggies, such as a favorite excursion or something they know they won't receive very frequently due to cost or inconvenience. Make a list of them, but don't forget to include ordinary perks. Aim for ten to fifteen privileges, with one-third being short-term, medium-term, and one-third being long-term. Consider the following scenario:

· Five short-term privileges are watching TV, playing video games, rollerblading, riding a bike, and having a buddy over after school.

· Staying up late, watching a special one-time TV show, spending the night at a friend's house, making cookies with Mom or Dad, and picking the family's supper menu are five middle-term privileges.

· Five long-term privileges include dining out, renting a DVD, throwing a party with friends, visiting an amusement park, and purchasing a sports-team shirt.

Make a list of chores to complete to earn chips. These can include simple personal tasks like brushing teeth and getting dressed, household chores like setting the table and taking out the trash, responsibilities like finishing homework and feeding the dog, and social behavior like not hitting a younger sibling or sharing toys with a visiting friend. Here are some essential guidelines:

Your child should help you make this list, but you should have the final word on what goes on it.

Use the current forms to remind yourself of the areas where your child's conduct is the most concerning. If washing and bathing are significant concerns, make a list of these personal responsibilities so that you can urge your kid to do them. If arguing with adults is a serious problem, make it a mission not to discuss with adults.

If you're going to make a list of things you don't want your child to do, be prepared to set a time limit to avoid those behaviors to earn points—for example, not arguing with an adult between breakfast and lunch.

Tell your child that you will occasionally—but not always—give them additional chips if they complete a task quickly or with a charming attitude.

Now assign the number of chips that each of these tasks can earn. Stick to one to three chips per work for younger children (ages four and five), maybe five for a substantial duty like tidying up all their toys in the family room or playroom. In appreciation of the greater complexity of responsibility, children aged six and seven can receive 1 to 10 points for each work.

Calculate how many chips the child will have to pay you for each specified privilege. This is all your responsibility. Begin by estimating the number of chips the child will earn on a typical day. I usually urge parents to spend roughly two-thirds of the chips made on privileges that will be used that day. That way, the child may preserve the remaining third for longer-term benefits. At this stage, accuracy isn't as crucial as it formerly was. Simply charge more chips for more significant incentives than everyday privileges, and try to be fair.

A sample chart for a five- or six-year-old child earning 30 chips each day on a weekday is as follows:

Benefit	Cost
TV (1/2 hour)	3
Video/computer games (1/2 hour)	3
Play outdoors Ride a bike	1
Choose a special dessert from the pantry	1
Stay up past bedtime with parents' permission	3
Have a friend over to play	5
Go to a friend's house to play	5
Rent a video game or movie	20
Go out for fast food (child chooses)	20
Spend the night at a friend's	30
Go to the movies	50
Buy a special toy/item	1 chip= 20 cents
Allowance: $2 per week	20

It's worth noting that the child's daily privileges require 20 chips. To be fair, keep it affordable when in doubt. To put it another way, if you're not sure about a price, go cheap, so the child sees it as reasonable. Before you do it, you'll know that it's a lot easier than it appears. You can get a good sense when you see how much your child can make on a regular day. Should a half-hour of TV cost 20 chips if a youngster earns 30 chips per day and we want to make sure he spends 20 of them on daily privileges? Obviously not.

However, it should not cost only one chip, as this would allow the youngster to watch 10 hours of television! Parents often allocate three chips each half-hour of television or Nintendo time.

Consider the first week as a shakedown voyage, in which you'll find out if your chip assignment is appropriate, and then you'll be free to adjust it as the program progresses. Some modifications will be necessary within the first week or so, but most families have found establishing a reasonable reward-privilege scale to be relatively simple. Also, keep in mind that your child may voice the changes made, so their thoughts might impact the activity.

Remind the kid of how chips may be won, such as performing a chore the first time you ask, as a bonus for having a pleasant mood, and for other positive conduct that you and the child haven't mentioned, such as not disturbing you. At the same time, you work or not interrupt you while on the phone.

Say you'll start the activity the next day after being confident the child understands it. The essential thing to remember is to be extremely generous with your chip giveaways. If the child cannot simply acquire chips and privileges, the plan will collapse immediately.

There will be no chips if there are no incentives. Thus there will be no motivation to act appropriately!

CHAPTER 7: TIME-OUT, MILD DISCIPLINE, AND MORE

The home token system you created in Step 3 is a valuable tool, but it isn't all-powerful. Most children, even those who appear to have entirely changed due to working for incentives, will revert to poor conduct for whatever reason. Other children will emerge from Step 3 to collaborate in various areas, but certain specific issues will continue. In any case, you'll need to find a new strategy to get them back on track. The "before" example demonstrates how easily the point system may mislead you into a false feeling of security by bringing about significant positive improvements.

Parents hope and pray that the motivation of prizes will convert their ODD child, and this is often the case. However, we've discovered that most honeymoons endure little more than three or four weeks. After that time, you should expect some disobedience at the very least. Remember that you haven't altered your child's inner wiring, and even your best attempts to prevent overloading the circuits will occasionally fail.

Suppose you aren't prepared for these relapses. In that case, old habits of interacting with your kid might resurface and draw you and your child into a cyclone of push-and-pull conflict so quickly that your newly restored connection appears to shatter around you.

Long-term behavioral issues, such as having difficulties getting along with other kids or failing to complete chores, might have a more subtle impact. Your incapacity to make progress in certain areas might make you feel powerless, and emotions of helplessness have a way of overshadowing the confidence you should gain over time as a result of your triumphs. You may not be able to fix every behavior problem with confident youngsters.

<u>Reintroduction Of Punishment</u>

Now the aim is to restore punishment sternly and progressively. Here's how you'll go about it:

When the child fails to complete a duty ordinarily awarded in the home token system, start subtracting points or chips.
Make a brief list of social infractions for which the child will also be penalized.

- Understand when and how to utilize a time-out.

- Choose one or two behavior issues you will use time-out.

Use the "fine twice, then isolate" rule. If the offense is repeated or continues, notwithstanding the initial fine, penalize the kid only once more before putting them in time-out.

Introducing Fines

Children who have been earning chips or points through the home token system will be understandably disappointed or upset if they are penalized for misbehaving. Still, after you've seen tangible advantages from encouraging compliance, you may start applying consequences for noncompliance. Simply deduct the number of points the kid would have gotten if they had obeyed the direction or completed the assignment. (If the child earns five points for making his bed in the morning, not making the bed means losing the five points already won as well as missing out on the five points that could have been earned.)

How much do you find the kid for throwing a tantrum, teasing her brother, lying to Mom and Dad, or violating some home rule if you aren't already compensating the child for these offenses? Basically, the more severe the misconduct, the harsher the punishment should be. Serious infractions should result in a loss of one-third or more of a child's average daily earnings. Taking away all of the child's payments for the day would be too harsh, while fines of only 5 to 10% of daily profits may be too little. Without bankrupting the child, about 25% to 30% of daily income should be enough to emphasize the point. If the same misconduct occurs again the next day, the fine will be increased by 10%. Remember the "Fine twice, then isolate" approach to avoid a punishment spiral.

Time-out

To prepare for this phase, locate a straight-backed chair, such as a dinette chair or an old-fashioned wooden school chair, and set it in a location where you can see the kid while going about your daily activities. The entrance, the center of a corridor, or a corner of the dining room or kitchen are all excellent places to put it. Ensure the chair is far enough away from the walls to prevent the kid from kicking them and that the child cannot reach anything to play with or mess with while seated.

Follow these procedures if you need to ask your child to perform something in the chosen category:

Issue the command (for example, "Tyler, put your filthy clothes in the laundry hamper"), using the rules for successful instructions acquired in Step 3.

If your kid does not begin to obey by the time you reach number one—after about five seconds—make direct eye contact with them and utilize body language that communicates your seriousness: "If you don't do as I say, you're going to sit in that chair!" adopt a stricter posture and stance, point your finger at the child, and speak louder than when you delivered the first instruction. ("You're going to sit on that chair if you don't put your clothes in the basket as I instructed!") Then indicate to your time-out chair.

Begin counting down from five once more. "You didn't do as I said. Therefore you're going to the chair," remark if you reach one again. ("You are going to the chair since you did not put your clothing in the basket as I requested.")

Then firmly grasp the child's wrist or upper arm and lead them to the chair.

"You sit there until I tell you can get up," you say, making sure your voice is loud and clear, so the child understands.

Allow one or two minutes in the chair for each year of the child's age—one minute for minor transgressions, two minutes for more serious ones. Go about your business to keep an eye on the child while the child is in time-out. Don't get involved in any conversations or disputes while the child is in time-out. Although the child is unlikely to sit quietly, you should disregard everything they say.

When the timer goes off, approach the child and tell them, "I'm not coming back to the chair until you're quiet." Then return to whatever you were doing when the child has been silent for around 30 seconds.

Return to the chair after the child has been silent for a few moments and ask whether the child is ready to accomplish what you requested. ("Are you ready to put your clothes in the basket, Tyler?" or, if the child has done something irreversible, "Are you ready to pledge you'll never strike Peter again?")

If the child agrees, make sure he follows through. (If the child strikes Peter again, return him to the time-out chair immediately, without order or warning.) If he doesn't, return him to the chair and begin again.

Start afresh with "All right, then you stay there until I say you can get up!" if the youngster says no. Repeat this process as necessary until the child follows your instructions.

"I enjoy it when you do what I ask," remark in a neutral tone of voice after the child has completed the task. Don't congratulate or thank the child for their cooperation. However, keep a close eye on the child to catch the following substantial-excellent behavior. When you do, remember to reward it, just as you did in Steps 2 and 3. This keeps the delicate balance of positive and negative in place. It also demonstrates that you don't detest your child and merely use time-out to punish misbehaving.

CHAPTER 8: USING TIMEOUT WITH MISCHIEVOUS BEHAVIOURS

You certainly already know if token penalties and timeouts are effective. Your ODD child's conduct should be improving in general, to begin with. Second, your child should be familiar with using timeouts. If you satisfy these conditions, you're doing well with punishment so far:

For each transgression, your child spends less time in the chair than he did at the start of Step 4. As discussed in the previous chapter, some children will have to remain in the timeout chair for a few hours the first time they are disciplined in this manner. Still, if the strategy proves effective, they will rapidly cooperate to reduce the time they are isolated from everything they desire.

Your child is starting to accept timeout as a punishment, resulting in fewer tantrums, complaints, and other fussing in the timeout chair. Many children react with tremendous righteous outrage to applying any punishment, so timeout can also be used.

Defiant children want what they want when they want it, and being separated from everything that interests and entertains them is an insult to them.

Your child is more likely to do what you ask in the time-out-targeted area. Did your daughter continue to work on her schoolwork for longer and longer amounts of time? Is your child interrupting your calls less frequently these days? Have you only had to instruct your child to put their things away twice today vs. ten times a week ago? Receiving a response to your initial request, and even better, having your child do what you want without being asked, are both evidence that you're implementing discipline successfully and fairly.

Your child is more likely to follow home rules. A peaceful home environment is primarily dependent on everyone adhering to household rules, such as "No slamming doors," "No cursing," and "No munching in the living room.". If your child is starting to follow this line due to you posting a list of rules and enforcing them, your house will likely be a safe haven than it has in the past.

You are much more confident in your parenting abilities. I don't need to tell you how disheartening it is to have your pleas disregarded, directives disobeyed, or your house transformed into a battleground. You should feel less powerless and more capable as a parent if you're receiving results from both punishment and praise—your child's conduct is starting to improve generally.

<u>Troubled spots</u>

"To show how little he appreciates our authority, my son's favorite weapon is to insult his father and me. His reaction to being put to timeout the other day was to execute a headstand in his chair. What chance do we have of making any progress this way?"

First and foremost, I hope you disciplined him for his actions during the timeout. The entire incentive/disincentive system will come apart unless you take the approach that every action taken by your child must be met with a response from you. Your child was attempting to provoke you by executing a headstand, and the only reward he should receive for his efforts is the unpleasant, consistent consequences you have established. Second, I hope you took advantage of the chance to joke about it—in private, of course.

I'm sure your child was attempting to be amusing, and as long as you don't let your sense of humor prevent you from carrying out your plan, you should take advantage of every opportunity to enjoy the relief that laughter provides. It's even better to show your child that you enjoy his humor while imposing the punishment.

"My child is just four years old, so it's difficult to determine how she feels about the timeout. She appears to be unhappy since she is quiet and unpleasant at times.

We saw her the other day giving her teddy bear a timeout for 'being naughty,' and her 'parent' manner was pretty severe. Aren't we doing more damage than good if that's how she views us?"

I seriously doubt it. In fact, your child's use of this tactic to punish her own charges clearly indicates that she believes timeout is beneficial.

This role-playing is followed by a change in behavior as judged by the five benchmarks mentioned before. If it isn't, there's a cause to be concerned about, and you should reconsider how you employ the timeout strategy.

Reread the previous chapters if you have any questions about your understanding of the procedure.

"When I was going to put my son in timeout last week, he would instantly promise to do what I asked. Should I let him comply so that I don't have to deal with the consequences of his failure to listen?"

No! After both your request and your following warning, you should count backward from five to one to allow the child some time to start complying. He should be placed in timeout if he hasn't started by then, even if he eventually decides to adhere later. Whether you don't, your child will learn to test the limits of your patience with every instruction you issue, simply to see if they can get away with it. You want him to obey your directions or heed your warnings. Even if it seems logical to let your child comply when he eventually relents on his way to timeout, you should go ahead and take the timeout nevertheless.

"Last week, while in timeout, Antonio repeatedly said that he despised and no longer loved me. He frequently stated this line. I already feel bad about his father leaving us last year and forcing me to divorce him; now, he is without a father to do things with. If he didn't love me anymore, I couldn't stand it."

Your emotions are very reasonable. However, this does not absolve you of your obligation as a parent to punish Antonio when he requires it. Children acknowledge our love and concern for them partly because we are willing to chastise them when they deserve it. Although they may not realize it at the time, they will learn to respect your honesty for taking the time to show them the proper and incorrect ways to conduct afterward.

Remember that Antonio may have felt your worries and concerns about punishing him because of your family background. And he's not beyond taking advantage of what he's picked up on you. So be sure your child isn't tricking you out of proper punishment by "pushing your emotional buttons" with statements he thinks will frighten you and make you give in. Later on, you might express your affection for him by paying closer and more positive attention to the nice things he undoubtedly does for you. But you must also demonstrate your love for him by keeping your commitments to chastise him if he disobeys you.

"Last week, Lucy was sent to timeout at least ten times. When I went to ask her whether she was ready to do what I requested, she looked at me furiously and simply answered, "No!" Is this a clue that my timeout strategy isn't working?" Certainly not. There can be times when your child is so angry that she didn't get her way or got out of doing something she didn't want to do that she will take longer to give in and agree to comply with you. "Fine, then you sit there until you decide to do what I requested," say to your child while she is in timeout and claims she is not ready to cooperate.

"OK. So I followed your instructions. When I saw Ivan striking his younger sister, I urged him to stop and counted backward from five. I cautioned him and counted backward from five as he continued to assault her. Then he came to a halt. However, he continued to attack her regularly this week. Nothing has changed except that I am constantly warning him and appear to be counting backward. He then stops, but he does it again later, so I have to warn him again. What exactly is going on here?"

It appears that you misinterpreted what we mentioned in the previous phase. We want our children to obey two types of rules. Our instructions and requests are an example of one kind. Picking up toys is an example of something we want a child to do when we ask them to do it.

"Household rules" are the other type. We don't want to keep repeating these.

It's a set of norms that govern how we want our children to act at all times. Other home rules might include not lying, stealing, swearing, using other people's valuables without permission, taking food without asking, and so on. A household rule is "no striking." Tell your child that he will face a timeout if he strikes his younger sister again. Every time he hits her after that, he is promptly placed in timeout. There are no instructions, no warnings, and no counting backward. Zip! Then it's time for a timeout. This should put an end to the hitting.

"Only a few times last week did we have to use a timeout with Sophie for not picking up her toys when instructed. However, I am concerned. She appeared depressed and moaned aloud that she couldn't seem to do anything correctly as she went to the chair for a timeout. She said that she deserved to be punished for all of her actions. She even said that she despised herself at one point. Is this typical?"

No, it isn't, but because something is uncommon doesn't mean it isn't a severe issue. It's conceivable that Sophie has realized that talking "depressed" like this and vocally berating herself for you irritates you. Sophie may be learning that verbal self-abuse earns your compassion and that you may be allowing her out of timeout sooner.

As a result, much as Antonio learned from his mother to declare he hated her since it seemed to bring him more sympathy and out of timeout sooner. Make sure you're not pushing your child to make certain verbal remarks to get sympathy and escape punishment.

On the other hand, Sophie may be clinically depressed if she is sad for more than 50% of the time for more than two weeks. If she says she wishes she were dead, you should take this very seriously. In any case, if her grief goes beyond being disturbed in timeout, you should seek professional help for her. This is especially true if depression runs in your family or the family of your husband.

Stop implementing the timeout approach if Sophie appears to be developing depression. Concentrate on your particular time, pay attention to her positive behavior, and use tokens as incentives for the beautiful things she performs for the time being. Also, get her professional assistance as soon as feasible.

"Last week, Rudy was put in timeout late in the afternoon because he refused to start his schoolwork when I asked him to. His father came in from work as he was seated in the corner.

'Hey, big guy, what's going on here?' his father remarked as he approached him. Did you get into your mother's hair? That's all right. 'Now that you've gotten your fill of that, let's go throw some baseballs around to warm up for your game tomorrow.' I was enraged. On the other hand, my husband claimed that Rudy is also his son and that he should be entitled to override my timeouts if he believes they are too long. "Who's the one who's right here?"

Yes, you are. Your husband made a mistake by interfering with your son's discipline. This can only teach Rudy that his father's judgment on punishment is essential and that your threats and discipline mean nothing. It would help if you talked to your spouse about this matter outside of Rudy's hearing. Let him know you realize that he is excited to see Rudy when he returns home and spends time with his son, but that everything should wait until Rudy's sentence is over. Make your husband aware that you will not interfere with disciplining Rudy if he needs to put him to timeout and that he should not interfere with yours. If this were a hockey game, Rudy's father would not walk down to the penalty box and tell his son he could leave before his punishment was over. He shouldn't do it in this place, either. That is a decision made by the referee. When you're disciplining, you're the referee, and it's up to you to decide when the timeout is up.

When your husband gets home the next time, Rudy is in timeout, greet him at the door, smile, and place your finger over your lips to signal that he must softly enter while Rudy is in timeout.

"Because he is agitated, my nine-year-old son will impulsively get out of the timeout chair. So, what should I do now?"

One father invented the following fascinating strategy: He and his son fashioned a "For Sale" sign out of plywood that they cut out using a jigsaw. The child preserved the placard alongside his favorite dirt bike. He misplaced a letter every time he got out of the timeout chair. He got a letter back if he managed to stay in the chair for the full timeout. The dirt bike would be sold if he lost all of the letters from the sign.

"After his timeout is finished, my child refuses to apologize for punching his sibling. So, what should I do now?"

For some children, making a vocal apology to a sibling is difficult and embarrassing. Instead, one family I know had the child write a short message to his sibling as a condition for the timeout to be lifted.

CHAPTER 9: THINK AHEAD AND ALOUD OF WHAT TO DO IN PUBLIC

Preparing ahead of time can help protect the uncontrollable from becoming unmanageable. Even though the context has changed, thinking aloud might help remind your child that you want the same good conduct you expect at home. If you inform your ODD child what to expect before going into a public location, the inevitable tiny indiscretions won't turn into nightmares. Many parents believe that teaching their children that good and bad behavior outside of the house has consequences prevents them from misbehaving in public. That, however, is contingent on the child's belief in your ability to stick to the rules you establish. When your child understands that you mean what you say at home, he will quickly realize that you will be just as trustworthy in other situations. In fact, many parents discover that after Step 5, all they need to do to prevent oppositional behavior in public is to establish the rules and the consequences ahead of time, and then occasionally praise (and chips or points) for good behavior as they go. They never require a timeout.

Here's a quick rundown of how Step 6 can help you get there:

Plan ahead of time. Anticipate the locations and moments when your child is likely to misbehave. Find the places and times when you are likely to lose your cool. Create reasonable expectations for your child's conduct in these settings, including rules to be followed, punishments for breaking them, and activities to keep your kid occupied while you're gone.

Speak your thoughts loudly. Before going into any public location, make sure your child understands the rules, consequences, and activities.

Apply the consequences when you're away from home, remembering to praise and reward frequently and inflicting acceptable discipline without embarrassment when necessary. Begin to use the same approaches at home for essential changes in the child's activities or special occasions.

<u>Where will your child in public is likely to create trouble?</u>

Take a few minutes to sit down with a piece of paper and make a note of locations, times, or situations when your child is likely to be disobedient or otherwise problematic.

Parents typically have a good idea of where their children are most likely to disobey the rules. Is your child obsessed with the supermarket's candy section? Is it tough for your child to avoid playing with everything in the toy store? Is it possible for your daughter to sit still and quietly at your place of worship? Is your son able to dine out decently? I'm sure you have a sizeable mental list of previous occurrences that alert you to potential issues.

Is it more straightforward to go on excursions at certain times of the day than at others? Maybe your daughter is OK with grocery shopping on a Saturday morning, but a spinning dervish if she is expected to keep her composure in any store after sitting at her desk all day at school. If you run an errand shortly before (or during!) their typical nap time, kids who still take naps will probably not be at their best. A 45-minute vehicle journey may be avoided if some active playing is arranged prior.

Other factors must also be considered. Is it preferable for your child to have a buddy or sibling to keep them company, or does friendship just give the child a potential "partner in crime"? Suppose your child is easily irritated or sensitive.

In that case, the exact location may have varied effects on her depending on the situation: Will a busy movie theater be more challenging to navigate than a deserted one?

Identifying embarrassing moments

Fear of humiliation can make it challenging to manage your child's conduct in public settings, so be prepared for your reactions to possible issues. Take another piece of paper and write down the spots where you're most likely to be humiliated by any "drama" your child creates. Some parents are unconcerned with misbehaving at the grocery store but are embarrassed if their child makes a noise at church. Others don't mind excessive noise or activity in public, but they can't stand rudeness. What irritates you the most? Whatever gives you worry or shame also compromises your capacity to manage your child calmly.

In some instances, more measures are required, such as additional incentives and distractions to encourage good behavior, as well as a further reminder of the rules before entering a public location. If they make you uneasy, you might not want to use them as test cases, at least not until you've earned some confidence in other scenarios.

Rest confident, though, that the success you've previously gained at home will transfer to other places without difficulty.

Credibility is a precious resource. Knowing that you will follow through on the consequences of misbehavior typically deters your child from behaving out in the first place. And if anything does go away, the disturbance should be far less than in the past, provided you're ready to move quickly and decisively. The best way to know for sure is to do it yourself, so let's get started.

How to operate in public

Explain the regulations to your child before allowing them to enter a public space. Stop immediately before entering the store, temple, restaurant, or other general location the first time out and explain the regulations to your child.

For a store, keep it brief and concise, like "Stand near, don't touch, and don't beg!" "Hands to yourself and don't talk!" can be appropriate for a place of worship. For older children, the rules can be more complicated—for example, in a restaurant, "Stay in your seat, don't touch your sister, and use your silverware"—but remember the idea of specificity. It's critical not to leave the rules up to the child's interpretation when you're out in public.

To be sure your child hears and understands the rules, have them repeat them back to you.

If you planned ahead, you'd have a good sense of what the regulations should be for places you frequently visit, such as grocery shops. You can tailor them to your own needs, but try to set some ground rules that you want your child to obey at all times in the shop. Then all you have to do the next time you go to the business is inquire outside, "What are the rules?" If your child forgets, rephrase them and have them repeat them.

Provide a monetary reward for cooperation. A set amount of chips or points from the token system is the most straightforward reward for your child, following the guidelines you've just outlined.

 They can be given out at intervals throughout the outing or all at once at the conclusion. If the latter, be sure to congratulate your child frequently for following the rules. If your kid is too young to use the home token system, you may bring a small bag of goodies with you to the shop and explain to the child that you'll be dispensing the rewards for cooperation while in public. If any of these suggestions is unfeasible, or if you need additional motivation, you may offer the youngster a different prize after the journey.

Explain what the consequences will be if you don't cooperate. Again, the most straightforward technique is to deduct tokens—"If you break the rules while we're having dinner, you'll lose 10 points"—but you should also be prepared to use a timeout. Many parents are hesitant to use a timeout in public because they believe it is impractical or disrespectful. I tell you that it is not impracticable because you definitely know enough about your surroundings to recognize a flat area. Timeout is also not a bad idea. No one likes to appear "mean" to onlookers, but taking your child away or yelling at him is far less harsh than letting him remain silently in a dull position. Most people will appreciate your attempts to keep your child from bothering them in public.

These tips will help you use timeout properly in public. Make sure that whatever penalty you tell your child will occur due to misbehavior is explicit, reasonable, and established ahead of time. Sean did not believe his mother would follow out her promise to take away his TV privileges for a week in the "before" scenario since the penalty was out of proportion to the "crime" and clearly sprang from emotion rather than rational reasoning. If you have to apply a consequence, do it right away, without repeating directions or regulations, and without bargaining with the child.

Negotiating and granting "one more opportunity" will only undermine your credibility when it comes to enforcing future penalties, just as it will at home.

Give your child a task to do. All children like assisting their parents, and they all prefer being assigned a practical chore that will keep them occupied during a trip or errand that you have planned rather than one that they have planned. Both you and your kid should find this a gratifying aspect of your travels. Take some time on the drive to the shop, if your child is old enough, to ask her for suggestions on how she might assist.

Have some of your own tips for a store—assisting you in finding anything on the shelves, marking items off your shopping list, carrying a small bag, or unloading your cart are just a few examples. While waiting for your meal to be served to the table at a restaurant, consider asking your stubborn youngster to assist your little sister by playing "I spy with my tiny eye." "As you wait for your dinner to arrive at the table. Ask your child to flip the pages of the hymnal for you at church. Make up your own story. Unstructured circumstances beg to be filled, and you may not always agree with your child's method of doing so. On the other side, activities arranged by parents have been shown to lessen oppositional behavior.

Begin by going out for two trial runs into the vast unknown. Choose two generally troublesome public places—perhaps one from your list of problematic settings for your child and one from your list of situations in which you're most uncomfortable with discipline—and plan a trip there only to use the strategy mentioned above. These rehearsals should demonstrate the effectiveness of the system. Nothing will be lost if you run into any problems: You won't get upset when shopping for supper or miss out on a much-needed meal out. You can start applying these measurements in the "real world" once you've had a pretty practical run-through.

Few examples to learn from

"I despise adding more regulations to my son's Christmas routine. He's so eager and cheerful, and I'm scared that being harsher on him now may backfire in the home. Do you have any suggestions?"

In fact, many families relax some of their usual norms and lessen the severity of the penalties during special occasions such as the holidays. Several couples concluded that the noise of a large family gathering necessitated a modified public-places approach to discipline in one of the parent groups we held around Thanksgiving.

They'd pick only two or three key restrictions (such as "no running in the house"), which they'd announce on Thanksgiving morning, just before the family arrived. Only those few rules would earn or lose tokens, not the standard household rules. Any timeout would likewise be reduced to the 30-seconds-per-year-of-age limit.

"We always travel by a full car when we go on a trip. When our son needs to serve a timeout in the car, where is everyone else meant to go?"

On this one, one family planned ahead: The parents bought a stack of magazines for their children—rock music and fashion magazines, comic books for their middle kid, and news publications for older kids—and stored them out of sight until a timeout was called. Then, when they arrived at a rest break, they surprised their son by pulling out the magazines and reading them in the front and rear seats while he sat in the cargo area of their SUV with nothing to do. For the following couple of hours, four minutes of this was enough to keep his behavior under control.

"Since timeouts and fines have worked for us at home, why can't we merely tell our child that any disobedience in public will result in punishment when we get home?"

This "wait till I bring you home" approach isn't appealing to most children. They expect you to respond quickly and decisively to misconduct, just as they want you to react swiftly and decisively to good behavior. Many stubborn children, especially those with ODD, cannot hold the notion of what will happen later in a way that will guide their conduct in the present.

That's why you've been using tokens and timeout at home: to reinforce the concept that every action you do has a constant, predictable response from you, whether good or negative. If you can't enforce sanctions right away for any reason, keeping track of violations in a notebook or placing hash marks on the child's hand will serve as an immediate response.

"I'm afraid I won't be able to impose a timeout during our religious sessions. I even find it amusing to speak about point penalties while I should be listening to the sermon, but when I try to put hash marks on my daughter's hand, she simply ignores me. What other options do I have?"

A more immediate reminder of what's in store at home can settle in and serve as a more effective deterrent. Some children find the visual reinforcement of seeing markings on the back of their hands sufficient. Others, however, do not.

I've found that displaying a photo of themselves on the timeout chair brings everything into focus. To make this tool work, show it to your daughter before you go to church and inform her that every hash mark she receives will result in a timeout when you arrive home.

"We've almost given on driving vacations due to the constant arguing in the back seat, but this year we have to travel hundreds of miles to attend a family reunion. What kind of reward do you propose for a child that is constantly misbehaving in the car?"

I'll share some brilliant advice from a family that had a similar problem: They informed their kid that for every 15 minutes that went without him disagreeing with anyone. On their long drive to see grandparents, he could earn 25 cents, spending during their stay. His parents claimed that the $20 they had to pay at their destination was the finest money they had ever produced.

CHAPTER 10: HELP YOUR CHILD BY HELPING THE TEACHER

You might not need to read this chapter right now if you're not getting calls or notes from your child's teacher and your child's academic performance is satisfactory. Some children never bring their defiant behavior to school, while others see such dramatic improvements in their behavior due to the steps you followed. Their excellent new behavior flows effortlessly into the classroom and onto the playground. Please read this chapter regardless so you won't be surprised if school troubles arise in the future.

The severity of your child's willful conduct will determine how likely they will have troubles in all situations. An exceedingly defiant child is expected to dispute with his teachers as often as he does with you or the lifeguard at the community pool;

An extremely defiant child is likely to disobey school regulations as well as home and social rules. For those whose behavior is more in the middle of the spectrum, the likelihood of defiance at school is determined by a variety of factors, including how well the school's level of structure matches your child's temperament, the types of social challenges the school presents, and the child-teacher relationship.

Your child's school day may be going swimmingly right now, but will it stay that way if a new teacher comes on board, your child graduates from elementary to middle school, or social turmoil erupts? Above all, remember that even in the circumstances with low levels of conflict, your defiant child has problems managing himself, adjusting, and being calm. As your kid matures and her schools provide new obstacles, they may exhibit lousy conduct.

If your child has been experiencing problems at school, I'm sure you've heard about it, and you can start using Step 7 immediately. If not, be ready to employ Step 7 if necessary, and remember that a "relapse" in behavior that shows itself at school does not always imply the honeymoon is gone. It might just be a glitch, easily rectified by following the steps outlined in this chapter. Most parents who seek help can stop using this strategy in a month or two.

Here's what you'll do, whether now or later: When you see poor behavior at school, talk to the teacher about the "daily school behavior report card." Together, you and your child may agree on the specific issues that need to be addressed, as well as how the teacher will report on your child's conduct daily.

The teacher will keep track of the child's conduct—in class, on the playground, or both—by sending home a behavior report card every day to assist them in overcoming behavior problems that are surfacing at school. Then you'll go through the card again, adding or deleting chips or points from the existing home token system, based on the "grades" the teacher has given the kid for that day.

Schedule a meeting with your teacher every few weeks to discuss your child's progress and go through their reports.

Plan to use the system for at least a few weeks, then transition from daily reports to two reports a week once a week or once a month, depending on how beneficial this stage has been, before phasing it out completely.

Cooperating with the teacher

To put this strategy into action, you'll need to gain the teacher's participation, which may be a delicate undertaking. Consider the bond you and your kid have built with this teacher so far before bringing up the idea of daily behavior report cards. Is there a sense of cooperation (or maybe a plot) to aid your child? Do you think the teacher sees you as a helpful parent who is realistic about your child's conduct and sensitive to the teacher's job? Have you been able to communicate well with one another? Is the teacher willing to help your child or frustrated by their persistent misbehavior? These elements may impact how well this idea is received when you offer it.

Also, keep in mind that all teachers have a lot of demands on their time and energy. It will depend on what you're asking adds to that list—at least at first. You'll need to communicate that you'll be doing the majority of the work, that you'll be responsible for enforcing sanctions, and that, most importantly, the teacher will benefit. Most teachers would jump at the chance to help your child, especially if they've already tried all they know to improve their conduct at school. In fact, you could present your strategy as a means to enhance the effectiveness of any in-class behavior modification technique that the teacher has tried and failed to work with. We've discovered that the behavior report card system is just as successful as, if not more effective than, these classroom behavior management tactics. It invariably improves the effectiveness of the in-class procedures.

Many of the approaches used by teachers to assist an oppositional defiant kid in continuing with the program were initially created for ADHD. Your child's teacher's simple actions might include sitting your child near the teacher's desk. Posting rules on signs and placing cards on the child's desk listing the regulations for desk work and having your child repeat the rules before a new period of activity begins. We educate instructors on employing techniques comparable to those used in this parent program, such as paying positive attention, issuing practical directives, and using a token system at school. However, these approaches are backed by the home token system. They typically receive a significant boost, as detailed in this chapter. One school rewarded students with points for good behavior, which could be redeemed for pencils, erasers, and other school supplies in the school store.

According to the parents of a 12-year-old child, the difficulty was that he didn't want pencils or anything else offered. They said that all he cared about after school was riding four-wheelers, sneaking smokes, and looking at "girly magazines" in the woods with his friends. Clearly, the school's behavior management program did not inspire the child to change his ways. However, tying it to the rewards, the approach worked at home.

If you get calls or notes concerning your child's conduct frequently, you'll have plenty of opportunities to discuss your strategy with the teacher. Otherwise, make an appointment with the teacher to discuss what you can do to assist the teacher with your child's conduct at school. Tell the teacher that what you're thinking of is one stage in a program that's helped you improve your child's behavior at home and in public. If you haven't discussed the program with the teacher all along, give them an outline of the home token system and the concepts you've chosen to control your child.

If the teacher agrees, ask if they would be willing to fill out the behavior rating forms before meeting with you, so you can both focus on your child's specific issue areas.

Few examples to learn from

"The teacher is so doubtful that any fresh attempt to control my son's conduct would be worth her time that she refuses to even meet with me to discuss it. What options do I have?"

First, try to explain to her that this program relies on you more than the teacher. The teacher has to keep track of behavior evaluations (which take only a few minutes each day) and leave the punishments to you. Point out that if your son's conduct is so awful, she is very certainly already paying close attention to what he's doing. Therefore, no extra monitoring is required.

Ask the teacher if she'd be prepared to test the program for a week, with the understanding that she'll reconsider if your son's conduct improves by Friday.

If she refuses to budge, see a school psychologist or guidance counselor. Likely, this teacher doesn't have enough time to focus on individual behavior control or lacks the educational foundation to comprehend the potential benefit. She could be more receptive to a request from another teacher.

Suppose the teacher is adamant about not cooperating. In that case, you might be able to implement the program in part by rewarding the behavior that you're already aware of: points for not receiving a phone call from the teacher for a certain number of days; points for not receiving a note about the child's behavior; and so on. You can punish your child for each detention or praise him if he avoids detention if his school offers a disciplinary program that includes, for example, detention for behavioral offenses and rule violations.

"How do we deal with a teacher that consistently sends home report cards that have unfair ratings?"

I suppose you feel the ratings are unjust, in which case you must exercise your discretion. If your child's cries of innocence are the source of your dissatisfaction with the ratings, speak with the teacher. You can inquire about the specifics of the misconduct. The success of this phase is contingent on everyone's reliability and fairness. Perhaps the teacher is overly zealous in the notion that a poor report card would motivate your child to change quickly and effectively. You've seen personally how positive reinforcement outperforms harsh punishment. You might describe the similarities in your program that highlight this concept if you can do so gently.

"Jimmy's teacher claims that she already fills out enough paperwork. She wants to assist but prefers to give us a daily update informally. Is this something we should agree to?"

You can, but it may be challenging to develop consistent and fair punishments unless you have a systematic manner of grading your child's conduct. We occasionally suggest keeping a notebook instead of using report cards. In some circumstances, a stenotype or spiral notebook is passed back and forth between the parent and the teacher. Each book contains notes on how the child is doing in that environment.

"My daughter is fighting us in any way she can, including not bringing her report card home at all. What are our options?"

You must apply severe punishment for failing to bring the report card home. Some parents believe that fining the child a total equal to the lowest conceivable report card grades is adequate. Others reprimand the youngster for the day, depriving her of the benefits commonly available through the token system.

"Katie is accustomed to receiving chips for excellent conduct and appears to be having difficulty linking what she did at preschool with the chips I give her when she comes home, resulting in the same pattern of ratings every day. To put it another way, we're not making much progress. Do you have any suggestions?"

For other children, the token system's consequences are simply too far away to be motivating. Do you remember to give praise and positive attention for reported excellent conduct as soon as the child arrives home before you attempt anything else? For many children, this is sufficient. If that isn't enough for your daughter, consider establishing a more tangible system of incentives, such as a favorite snack after school, more television time, a trip to the petting zoo for a week of getting high grades, and so on.

"This curriculum is working too well for my youngster. He's accumulating so many points that he can't possibly use them all on privileges. What should we do differently?"

This is something I've heard before. Some children become so enamored with the newfound income that they stop attempting to gain points outside of school, and their home conduct suffers as a result.

In this instance, the best thing to reassess is how much each reward or privilege on the child's list costs. Then either add some new benefits that need more points to obtain or increase the worth of existing prizes so that the child is motivated to earn more points every day.

"My daughter's main issue is that she forgets to write down her homework assignments. We've run out of ideas because she's progressed in every other area except that. Help!"

Make an assignment journal on the back of the report card. As the day progresses, ask the teacher to have your kid write the tasks on the reverse of the card. Before grading the child's conduct and initialing the card, the teacher should verify the assignment for correctness at the end of each session. When the child returns home, you can be confident that you and the child have a detailed record of the homework thymus to be completed.

"I have my suspicions. My son is now getting 1's and 2's on everything. Does that seem likely?"

It's absolutely feasible, but it's unlikely given the nature of behavioral change. I hate to admit it, but students have been known to input their own ratings and counterfeit their teachers' initials by using substitute teachers and other loopholes. That's one of the reasons you should set up meetings with the teacher—it's an excellent opportunity to show her the report cards and see whether she filled them out herself.

"Why does my daughter make the same mistakes over and over again, despite knowing the consequences?"

The time gap between school conduct and the sanctions enforced at home is the most significant hurdle to profiting from these report cards. Some children, particularly those with attentional issues associated with ADHD, have difficulty retaining the behavior-consequence link. Making the same mistake and experiencing the same consequence numerous times requires more reinforcement to make it stay. The variation in the environment can sometimes destroy the mental link that children need to urge themselves to perform correctly.

Discussing with your kid how she may handle a difficult circumstance differently the next day provides her with a plan to follow, but can she keep that goal a day later at school? Many people cannot do so. Therefore, I advise you to remind your daughter about behaving in these situations before sending her off to school.

"My son's teacher says he's doing well in class, but once he's out on the playground, he appears to loosen up and break all the rules. Why Isn't his report card encouraging him?"

At recess, all children need to blow off steam. It's very uncommon for well-behaved kids to have a misbehavior problem during this time off. The trouble for your son might be the change of scenery: He just forgets the rules when there is less structure. Before recess, ask the teacher to adopt the "think ahead, think aloud" procedure: The instructor should remind your kid of the recess regulations, noting that they are mentioned on the report card, reminding him that he is being monitored by the playground monitor, and instructing him to hand over the report card to the monitor.

CHAPTER 11: DRIVING TOWARDS A BETTER AND BRIGHTER FUTURE

The last phase is a huge step forward for parents with ODD children. This is the point at which you move toward a bright future for your kid and your family. By now, you should have plenty of proof that the previous strategies were wisely spent and that what you've learned together has far-reaching implications beyond your house. Getting along with you better naturally aids your child in getting along with others. Being able to obey rules and act responsibly at home offers your child the confidence and ability to lead a successful life in the real world. You should now be able to look forward to the future with renewed optimism, knowing that your child's tendency for misbehavior will not prevent them from growing into a happy and healthy adult.

That isn't to say that your work is done. You can remove the token systems and school behavior report cards that have aided your efforts so far—this chapter will show you how to do so wisely—but the ideas woven throughout this program should always guide your parenting.

Many parents have discovered that it's too simple to revert to old destructive behaviors when dealing with a defiant child. As a result, one of the most important goals of this last phase is to provide you with a way to analyze your own conduct when your child's behavior appears to be deteriorating.

Current status

Your relationship with your child should now be on a more level keel, assuming you spent at least two months on the mentioned strategies and stuck with each step for as long as it took to see some change. At the very least, a measure of long-term peace should have settled over your previous battleground. If the forms don't indicate a significant difference in your child's behavior after you've used all the strategies, keep using all of the tactics you've learned until you believe things are improving. Then complete the paperwork to check whether they agree.

In general, we consider improvement to be a drop in scores of 30 to 50 percent from your previous results. Stay with the program a bit longer if you haven't gone that far. If you haven't noticed any progress in the first two months, I recommend sticking with the strategies for another month.

If nothing has changed by then, seek professional help for your child.

<u>Phasing out tokens, fines, and report cards</u>

If your kid is presently using the daily school behavioral report card system, you must also use the home token system, even if your child does not appear to require that reward for excellent conduct at home. As a result, your priority should be to phase out the report card system.

After two weeks of school with good results, consider weaning your child from the report card program. Request that the teacher fills out the cards only on Wednesdays, reporting on conduct from Monday to Wednesday, and Fridays, reporting on behavior from Thursday to Friday. You can have the teacher move to Fridays only when your child has gone two weeks without any 4s or 5s, with the card reporting on the entire week's conduct. Suppose your child has improved at school due to a behavior modification strategy only to regress later. In that case, it's a good idea to use monthly report cards for a time before eliminating them. Otherwise, you may just call the teacher once a month to check in.

Tell your child that getting rid of the report cards does not imply the teacher will stop paying attention to their conduct. In fact, if the instructor gives you any bad feedback about your child's conduct, you should reintroduce the daily report cards. You might try eliminating the home token system on which the report cards are based after your kid behaves satisfactorily at school without a behavior report card. Tell your child that the token system will be suspended for a few days if they act correctly at home. Of course, you'll continue to monitor the child's conduct, and you should reassure the child that getting privileges will still be contingent on the child's good behavior. The only thing lacking is the accumulation of chips or recording points. If your child's conduct deteriorates without the official home token system, just reinstall it, just like you would in the school system.

Avoiding the trouble

When your child reverts to prior misbehavior or comes up with a new form of disobedience, the home token system isn't your only option. In fact, reverting to the token system right away may not be the wisest course of action in the event of a crisis.

First, attempt to figure out why your child is behaving out once more. With all of the changes that children go through as they develop, it's not uncommon for them to confront obstacles that they can't handle with their newfound calm. Know your child and what's going on in their life to help both of you overcome these obstacles.

To put it another way, pay attention! Once you feel your child's conduct is under control, it's tempting to relax your guard. Peer pressures, advancement from grade to grade and school to school, physical maturity, and other aspects of a child's life need your attention and understanding. Keep an eye on what's going on in your child's life. Predict issues based on what you already know about their strengths and limitations. Prepare ahead of time and speak your thoughts aloud!

You probably already use this helpful strategy when your child's everyday life is about to undergo substantial changes. When overnight visitors arrive, a party is planned, the family goes out to dinner, and so on—but you can also use it when more significant changes are predicted. Is your child set to start kindergarten for the first time? Is your daughter's closest friend relocating to another city? Is a teacher for your child being replaced during the school year?

Don't only consider the changes that will directly affect your child. Keep in mind that changes impacting the rest of the family or other aspects of the child's life are likely to affect him as well. Are you and your spouse having marital issues or contemplating a divorce? Do you have a new baby on the way? Is there anyone in your family who suffers from a chronic illness? Are you beginning a new career or returning to school?

Also, keep in mind that your child may be stressed by more than just the ostensibly unfavorable developments. A parent's huge work promotion, a relocation to a new, larger house, a fourth-grade transition to the "gifted" group, or a puppy present from Grandma may all send your child into a tizzy, just as household strife, loss, or disappointment might.

Be mindful of circumstances and activities that are frequently annoying to your kid, in addition to anticipating the impact of significant shifts in their life. Make a note of places, situations, persons, or other variables that frequently cause your kid to act defiantly. Make a mental note of these issue locations and commit to thinking ahead and thinking aloud to avoid problems when these elements eventually enter your child's world.

<u>Manage the problems</u>

Several parents have complained about the following issues throughout the years. Some of these may apply to your child as well.

Long wait times. "We arm ourselves with lots of engrossing activities and arrange for extra incentives for Nick's patience anytime we have to go to a doctor's or dentist's office or even wait in line for a popular movie," his father stated. "When we go to the grocery and observe huge queues at the checkout, we attempt to come back later. When we're caught off guard and can't get out of waiting for anything, I usually keep a little bag of chocolate-covered raisins in my pocket, which Nick adores, as a prize for every five minutes of patient waiting."Making a new friend "When Kevin gets home and begins chattering nonstop about a new friend he's made, I know there's going to be problems. When he really wants to impress someone, he goes beyond and becomes aggressively demanding, so we try to 'think aloud' and gently remind him of the ground principles of social interaction—no shoving, no name-calling, and so on. We come up with minor scenarios to help Kevin predict difficulty because he enjoys what-if games: 'What if Tony came over to play and inquired about riding your new bike? How would you react?'

Social gatherings with a large number of people "Jess is OK one-on-one. She's typically fine when there are an even number of girls so they can pair up (three is usually a problem), but in a large, uncontrolled group, she may completely unravel. Class time is nice because of the framework, but Brownies just didn't work for her. We don't want Jess to miss out on all of these great things. So we talk to the adults to pull Jess out for a break. She finds that taking a little pause helps her from being too worked up."

"There will be visitors." Alice has a hard time adjusting to changes in her schedule, such as having overnight guests. We tried to come up with a uniform set of 'company's coming' rules for these regular occasions — both Peter and I have huge families spread throughout the country — but after a time, we found his misbehavior varied depending on who's coming to visit. When he's with her grandparents, he reverts to wheedling and tantrums since she knows they're softies who would give in to many of his demands. When it comes to his relatives, he's more inclined to be pushy, if not physical. So now we have two sets of corporate rules, and we focus on a few specific actions in each: When relatives visit, we award a lot of points for not striking or bossing the other kids, and we deduct a lot of violations.

The birth of a new child." Because I already had two children, I assumed I knew what to anticipate from sibling rivalry, but I'm pleased our group discussed how new infants influence oppositional defiant children. The preparations I was able to make based on their experiences were highly beneficial to Ana during what could have been a difficult transition period. First, I assured Ana that special moments would be sacred. I cuddled her and promised that we'd always have a particular time together, even if it meant keeping the sleeping baby in a cart. We also discussed how aggravating new infants could be and came up with a short set of new house rules for our new arrival. 'No shouting at the baby,' 'no striking the baby,' and 'no entering the baby's room when the infant is asleep' are some of the rules. Ana would receive five additional points for following each of these guidelines for the day during the first month and ten bonus points if she followed one of them for a week. We decided to post a sign on the nursery door with the words' Zzzzz' on it to signal that the baby was sleeping to avoid disagreements ('But, Mom, I didn't know the baby was sleeping).

There have been times when Ana and I have acted out when the baby has been unhappy, but in general, our planning has proven to be really beneficial.

She told me the other day, sincerely, that if the baby wanted to, she might play with us during our special moments."

What to do when the child's oppositional defiant behavior return

"Think ahead/think aloud" involves more than simply explaining the rules and penalties to your kid before a change. It also consists in devising a strategy for dealing with your child's misbehavior. Here's what we suggest:

If your kid begins to misbehave regularly, get a notepad or pad and write down the facts of the problem. It must include what your child is doing wrong (what rule is being broken). It also includes when, where, and what you are doing to control the behavior.

Keep this journal for a week or more, noting what the child's behavior repeats and what new twists appear.

See if there are any indications regarding how you're "behaving." If you examine the situation objectively, you may discover that the problem is being created by — or exacerbated by — your return to unpleasant old ways of disciplining your child: over punishment, pressure, favor-seeking, inconsistency, unfairness, or a lack of specificity. Ask yourself the following questions as you go over your records.

Take the following steps to modify your own behavior: Give yourself a couple of days to see whether the problem starts to fix itself using the skills you've learned.

If not, tell your child what you expect of them regarding the misbehavior. From now on, you may not leave your desk until your homework is completed". You can also say there will be no more swearing in the house. Set up a token system to reward compliance with the rule you've just explained. Make sure you're paying attention so you can hand away tokens when they're earned.

From now on, impose a time-out whenever the misconduct occurs. Keep taking notes until the issue appears to be resolved. If none of this helps, you might need to seek expert assistance.

My final request…

Being a smaller author, reviews help me tremendously!

It would mean the world to me if you could leave a review.

If you liked reading this book and learned a thing or two, please let me know!

It only takes 30 seconds but means so much to me!

Thank you and I can't wait to see your thought.

CONCLUSION

Congratulations! You've just finished the book that contains all the valuable information needed to help your child with oppositional conduct disorder. If everything went well, you should have seen changes in your child's behavior, your stress levels as a parent, and your child's ability to perform tasks and meet others' expectations. You could even discover that the advantages have extended to your other children.

Most parents say that these strategies have given them a renewed sense of self-awareness and confidence in their ability to face the future and any behavioral challenges considering their ODD children. You deserve a lot of credit for the time, effort, and perseverance you put into helping your ODD child, and you deserve the confidence you've gained. You have encouraged your child to be more responsive to direction, more trustworthy in carrying out day-to-day responsibilities. You have made him more positive and effective in interactions with others by doing your best to change yourself in how you interact with your child and manage your child's behavior. As a parent, you can't do much better than that for your oppositional defiant child.

Resources

Hamilton, S., & Armando, J. (2008). Oppositional defiant disorder. *American family physician*, 78(7), 861-866.

Burke, J. D., Loeber, R., & Birmaher, B. (2002). Oppositional defiant disorder and conduct disorder: a review of the past 10 years, part II. *Journal of the American Academy of Child & Adolescent Psychiatry*, 41(11), 1275-1293.

Drabick, D. A., & Gadow, K. D. (2012). Deconstructing oppositional defiant disorder: Clinic-based evidence for an anger/irritability phenotype. *Journal of the American Academy of Child & Adolescent Psychiatry*, 51(4), 384-393.

Riley, M., Ahmed, S., & Locke, A. (2016). Common questions about oppositional defiant disorder. *American family physician*, 93(7), 586-591.

Greene, R. W., Biederman, J., Zerwas, S., Monuteaux, M. C., Goring, J. C., & Faraone, S. V. (2002). Psychiatric comorbidity, family dysfunction, and social impairment in referred youth with oppositional defiant disorder. *American Journal of Psychiatry*, 159(7), 1214-1224.

Lanza, H. I., & Drabick, D. A. (2011). Family routine moderates the relation between child impulsivity and oppositional defiant disorder symptoms. *Journal of abnormal child psychology*, 39(1), 83-94.

Rey, J. M., Walter, G., Plapp, J. M., & Denshire, E. (2000). Family environment in attention deficit hyperactivity, oppositional defiant and conduct disorders. *Australian & New Zealand Journal of Psychiatry*, 34(3), 453-457.

Matthys, W., Van Goozen, S. H., Snoek, H., & Van Engeland, H. (2004). Response perseveration and sensitivity to reward and punishment in boys with oppositional defiant disorder. *European child & adolescent psychiatry*, 13(6), 362-364.

Luman, M., Sergeant, J. A., Knol, D. L., & Oosterlaan, J. (2010). Impaired decision making in oppositional defiant disorder related to altered psychophysiological responses to reinforcement. *Biological Psychiatry, 68*(4), 337-344.

Greene, R. W., Biederman, J., Zerwas, S., Monuteaux, M. C., Goring, J. C., & Faraone, S. V. (2002). Psychiatric comorbidity, family dysfunction, and social impairment in referred youth with oppositional defiant disorder. *American Journal of Psychiatry, 159*(7), 1214-1224.

Cavanagh, M., Quinn, D., Duncan, D., Graham, T., & Balbuena, L. (2017). Oppositional defiant disorder is better conceptualized as a disorder of emotional regulation. *Journal of attention disorders, 21*(5), 381-389.